C A P S T O N E

Stay Smart!

Smart things to know about... is a complete library of the world's smartest business ideas. Smart books put you on the inside track to the knowledge and skills that make the most successful people tick.

Each book brings you right up to speed on a crucial business issue. The subjects that business people tell us they most want to master are:

Smart Things to Know about **Brands & Branding**, JOHN MARIOTTI

Smart Things to Know about **Business Finance**, KEN LANGDON

Smart Things to Know about **Change**, DAVID FIRTH

Smart Things to Know about **Customers**, ROS JAY

Smart Things to Know about **E-Commerce**, MIKE CUNNINGHAM

Smart Things to Know about **Knowledge Management**, TOM M. KOULOPOULOS & CARL FRAPPAOLO

Smart Things to Know about **Strategy**, RICHARD KOCH

Smart Things to Know about **Teams**, ANNEMA'

D1374264

You can stay **Smart** by e-mailing us at **capstone_publis**̶̶̶̶̶ keep you up to date with new Smart books, Smart updates, a smart newsletter and Smart seminars and conferences. Get in touch to discuss your needs.

C A P S T O N E

Smart

THINGS TO KNOW ABOUT

E-Commerce

MIKE CUNNINGHAM

Copyright © Mike Cunningham 2000

The right of Mike Cunningham to be identified as the author of this work has been asserted in accordance with the Copyright, Designs and Patents Act 1988

First published 2000 by
Capstone Publishing Limited
Oxford Centre for Innovation
Mill Street
Oxford OX2 0JX
United Kingdom
http://www.capstone.co.uk

All rights reserved. Except for the quotation of short passages for the purposes of criticism and review, no part of this publication may be reproduced, stored in a retrieval system, or transmitted, in any form or by any means, electronic, mechanical, photo-copying, recording or otherwise, without the prior permission of the publisher.

CIP catalogue records for this book are available from the British Library and the US Library of Congress

ISBN 1-84112-040-5

Typeset in 11/15 pt Sabon by
Sparks Computer Solutions Ltd, Oxford
http://www.sparks.co.uk
Printed and bound by
T.J. International Ltd, Padstow, Cornwall

This book is printed on acid-free paper

Substantial discounts on bulk quantities of Capstone books are available to corporations, professional associations and other organizations. If you are in the USA or Canada, phone the LPC Group for details on (1-800-626-4330) or fax (1-800-243-0138). Everywhere else, phone Capstone Publishing on (+44-1865-798623) or fax (+44-1865-240941).

For my wife Sally
and my children Ian, Terri, Ryan and Alasdair.
For their continuous love and support,
and their understanding of Internet time

and

the staff, clients and business partners of
the Harvard Computing Group,
for the opportunity to learn and work
in the most exciting business sector on the planet.

Contents

What is Smart?

The *Smart* series is a new way of learning. *Smart* books will improve your understanding and performance in some of the critical areas you face today like *customers, strategy, change, e-commerce, brands, influencing skills, knowledge management, finance, teamworking, partnerships.*

Smart books summarize accumulated wisdom as well as providing original cutting-edge ideas and tools that will take you out of theory and into action.

The widely respected business guru Chris Argyris points out that even the most intelligent individuals can become ineffective in organizations. Why? Because we are so busy working that we fail to learn about ourselves. We stop reflecting on the changes around us. We get sucked into the patterns of behavior that have produced success for us in the past, not realizing that it may no longer be appropriate for us in the fast-approaching future.

There are three ways the *Smart* series helps prevent this happening to you:

- by increasing your self-awareness

- by developing your understanding, attitude and behavior

- by giving you the tools to challenge the status quo that exists in your organization.

Smart people need smart organizations. You could spend a third of your career hopping around in search of the Holy Grail, or you could begin to create your own smart organization around you today.

Finally a reminder that books don't change the world, people do. And although the *Smart* series offers you the brightest wisdom from the best practitioners and thinkers, these books throw the responsibility on you to *apply* what you're learning in your work.

Because the truly smart person knows that reading a book is the start of the process and not the end ...

As Eric Hoffer says, "In times of change, learners inherit the world, while the learned remain beautifully equipped to deal with a world that no longer exists."

David Firth
Smartmaster

Preface

As managers and professionals in organizations today we are faced with change as a normal way of life. We are in a world that expects us not only to know what is going to happen next, but to have predicted the solution so we are ready to exploit change when it comes. Change is at the very heart of every aspect of e-commerce, but how do we get our heads around what e-commerce even means, let alone what it means to us? We seem to have as many definitions of the subject as there are vendors and suppliers in the marketplace.

This book provides guidance for you to navigate these waters. Over the course of the next eight chapters, you should start to understand the relationship between the complex elements of e-commerce and how they affect an organization and a marketplace.

E-commerce is not just technology, it's a way of doing business differently. A fundamental goal of this book is to help you understand the relationship between the technology components and the other things that have to change in an organization to support it. For many years I have been a frustrated participant in the computing industry, frustrated because the industry has made it so hard for others to make good decisions about technology and how to use it effectively. The industry has always focused on just one aspect of the problem. The vendors tout the technology and what it can do, consultants have espoused re-engineering while ignoring the technology components, and as a result there are many confused technologists and managers out there.

The terrible failure rates of most information technology projects continue to scare the best of us. I believe that one reason the failure rate is so high is related to the poor integration of business goals, work process change and technology in determining plans. We also have a tendency to acquire technology in the same way that we did in the 70s and 80s, using requests for proposal and long buying cycles. By the time we reach a conclusion, the technology has changed twice, and so may the marketplace. *Smart Things to Know About E-commerce* takes aim at these problems. First, we are going to arm you with the necessary information to understand where the "bodies are buried" before you start out on your journey. Understanding the technology, its impact on the organization and the importance of new business models should help clear the way forward. You will not become an expert in any one of the areas covered within, but you will be smarter about all of them. You will understand their importance and relevance to the e-commerce marketplace. We also hope that you will be better able to determine which types of systems are most relevant to your needs.

As nothing helps us succeed like success, I have taken many examples, quotes and references from others who have been e-commerce pioneers and visionaries.

Building a guide for e-commerce strategies is rather like producing a history course at the same time that the war is raging in the field. It is difficult, particularly when the battlefield and tactics are changing frequently. We must learn on a day-to-day basis, and need to take what we have learned to battle the next day. I apologize for starting this book with a warfare analogy. However, I think that it is naïve for us to look at e-commerce as anything other than business warfare. There, now I have your attention. But if you're smart you'll think about it for a moment. We have never been faced with tools and strategies that can give us direct access to so many consumers and customers in such a short time. Likewise, your competitors have never had such easy, direct access to your client base. Electronic information about all of us is being bought and sold to a broad range of companies targeting our purses and wallets. Similarly, the trends occurring in business to business e-commerce have already had a staggering impact on the marketplace. *Smart Things To Know About E-commerce* will help you understand where to look for new e-commerce strategies and solutions that address the complex new world that is facing us. We can ignore what is going on out there, or we can embrace it. Regardless of whether you decide to embrace or ignore, understanding how and why these systems are important could be one of the most important business issues you will ever face. Whether you are reading for the development of your career, to improve your organization's operations, or are considering starting your own company, this book will help you define and refine your plans.

This book will help you learn about e-commerce and the changes it brings. It will help you get ready for it, and tackle it more effectively. We are really faced with two options, adopt or become a victim. If you do not want to change, then don't do anything. But realize that your competition is changing, and they will either force you to change against your will or they will force you into extinction. I say this not to scare you. It's just that a well executed e-commerce business can create value and absorb marketshare at rates that we have never seen before.

Used effectively, e-commerce has power that is much greater than the number of people in the company. E-commerce can leverage intellectual property in a way we could not imagine a few years ago. It delivers a level of marketing capacity previously limited to the very largest corporations, those with the biggest brand and budget capabilities. E-commerce allows targeting of individuals and their needs in a way that has been the bailiwick of niche markets and small players. The internet and e-commerce can let a company have both.

I have spent most of my career focusing on the application of computing technology to solve practical business problems. Sometimes I have been involved with building new and complex software systems. In other cases, I have helped organizations integrate their work process and technology solutions in a common framework. In each situation, I have tried to link the technology to the business need. Without this primal connection, we have a tendency to produce useful weapons but ones that are focused on the wrong target. This book will help you improve your aim.

I also continue to be surprised about the lack of tools out there to help the individual business owner, the rising middle manager and the executive to understand how to apply technology to business problems. *Smart Things To Know About E-commerce* will help you develop strategies and programs specifically for e-commerce business problems.

What is all the fuss about?

Rarely has a subject been more touted than e-commerce in recent years. This is not surprising really, because e-commerce is all about money. Lots of money. A combination of vast sums of money, the internet and a strong economy in the United States has riveted our attention on this topic. The Initial Public Offerings, wild company valuations, the rocketing stock market, and the increasing demand for information professionals have contributed to a near frenzy in the development of e-commerce systems. Have we all gone crazy, or have we truly found a new place and way of doing business in cyberspace? Will it change the way that we work? Will it change work itself? As this market develops right under our noses, it is sometimes difficult to really see what is happening. However, it is not as complex as it sounds. The foundation for e-commerce includes the following principles:

- collecting money from consumers

- collecting money from business partners (supply chain)

- improving the productivity of current processes

- developing and supporting new automated processes

- changing how you deal with existing customers

- changing how you deal with new customers.

Smart quotes

Now this is a knife.

Paul Hogan (comparing his 6-inch bowie knife to the switchblade of his attacker in the movie *Crocodile Dundee*)

Almost all e-commerce strategies and programs can be attached to these principles. In fact, if you cannot connect them, then it is probably not e-commerce that you are looking at, but some other internet-based scheme that is unlikely to be worth pursuing.

Smart Things to Know about E-commerce is written for those individuals and managers who face these changes and challenges. It will help you become better armed to deal with them, and understand the important relationship between e-commerce and our organizations today, and in the future.

Although this is a very technical subject, the function of the components and how they work together is not so complex. *Smart Things To Know About E-commerce* will not make you a technical expert, but you will have enough knowledge to identify the components and their relationship with the other important elements that make e-commerce systems work.

Smart Things To Know About E-commerce is not intended to be a change management handbook. Rather it will provide you with guidelines to help you find your own solutions. My own experiences with e-commerce have taught me to continue to be inquisitive, open and receptive to new ideas. As a consultant in this industry, I am frequently asked to comment, revise or validate business ideas and strategies in this market. The creative mind of an entrepreneur with a new idea, why they dreamt it up in the first place and how they plan to bring it to market is often a joy to behold.

There are many ways to build a business with e-commerce as the hub. Sometimes we need to consider fairly radical ideas and business models to make it work. Other solutions demand large changes in how we work with our partners. Keeping an open mind is one of the greatest assets in the development of systems. You cannot afford to become locked in by one technology, a single strategy or the marketplace as it exists today. The days of the business model that can be predicted for five years without change are dead (aside from nationalized industries that control the marketplace and demand).

Another factor that really affects our thinking in e-commerce is *time*. Successful managers assume that they have very little time to get to market. They also assume that their enemy is working on the same thing and has twice as many resources applied to the problem.

We need to be ready for change in our thinking, our strategy and our business plans. An open mind and readiness for change may be the most important assets we can bring to the table in an e-commerce strategy. Knowing our market is a substantial third to these factors.

The strategies included in this book are based on practical experience and a successful record of accomplishment in developing, implementing and creating value for organizations using e-commerce systems. Every element of the book is touched by the tactical consulting programs and systems used at the Harvard Computing Group, Inc. I am deeply grateful to the staff there for their input in the development of this book. I would like to pay a special thanks to Scott Helmers for his editorial and technical assistance and my wife for her continuous support and encouragement.

I hope that *Smart Things To Know About E-commerce* will make you more aware of the technology components that will influence your e-commerce strategies. You should be able to see more clearly how to build a plan for a system and see how your current business processes and a potential e-commerce solution can work together. I also hope that you will find the extensive quotations, references and examples of other systems useful in your quest. After all, we all need to see the tactics that the successful generals are using if we are to have a chance of winning our own battles.

Mike Cunningham
December 1999

1

The Internet and E-commerce Evolution

Understanding what the Internet is and how it is affecting our lives is not an easy task. We cannot compare the way it is changing us to other historical industrial and social change. The Internet provides us a framework for business, yet we can also play games. We can shop and we can learn, find partners and do research, watch TV and gamble. Many of the things we do in our everyday life we can do on the Internet. In a word, the Internet means change, we just do not know exactly how much change. The overnight success that we know as the Internet celebrated its thirtieth birthday in 1999. In terms of history however, we have to consider the Internet a youngster, a youth with an interesting heritage, one worth reviewing.

Some Smart readers may already be familiar with the story of the Internet and how it works. If you're one of these you're welcome to skip this chapter and go straight to Chapter 2.

The evolution of the Internet

Despite the fact that the Internet has only been popular in the past few short years, it is difficult for us to imagine a world without its presence. The daily barrage of new sites, special deals, business offers and applications changes that meet us headlong are mind-boggling. The Internet appears magical and mystical, friendly and scary, warm and dangerous at the same time. We want our kids to use it for research, but are wary of the consequences of them travelling to unplanned or undesired destinations. The Internet has become a center for both commerce and global swindles in what seems only an instant of time.

The US Government started the process when they laid the framework for the Internet in the late 1960s. In particular, the Department of Defense (DoD) decided to fund a network of computers that would all talk the same language. They wanted to connect researchers, government workers and defense contractors (i.e., those companies providing systems and data to government agencies). As most brands of computers at this time employed very different rules for communication (known as protocols), DoD decided to develop a vendor-independent suite of protocols. The new network was named ARPAnet after the Advanced Research Projects Agency within DoD that provided the funding.

Early ARPAnet protocols were replaced in the 1970s with the now very popular TCP/IP protocol suite. The features in these protocols permitted reliable transmission of data from any one computer connected to the ARPAnet to any other computer on the net. The ARPAnet provided the foundation for the Internet as we know it today.

Another major US government requirement was to ensure that the system was secure and would allow continued communication between these sites and computers in the case of nuclear attack. Therefore, the serious requirement of redundancy of the Internet was built into the system from the word go.

As the Internet evolved from a military focus towards non-military use, electronic mail became the first killer application for commercial users. The ability to communicate electronically using this medium became very popular, very quickly. Over this same period of time, office productivity applications were developing. Firms such as WANG were making millions from specialized computers providing office functions across a proprietary network. These networks were very useful for medium to large-scale organizations, but still not affordable to smaller businesses.

> *Smart things to say about e-commerce*
>
> *Redundancy:* instant failsafe backup of computer systems to ensure that they continue to operate effectively in the case of a single or multiple points of failure.

The role of the personal computer

Enter the personal computer: Here was the device that was going to make a difference. Suddenly, the power of medium size mini-computers had scaled to a new level. The early 1980s saw the entry of the first serious PC products to market, and the adoption rate was phenomenal. In the United States, early adopters purchased computers partially as a statement of their liberation from internal IT purchasing policy, further exaggerating this trend. Departments could now make decisions about computers without being bogged down in months of bureaucratic effort involving the MIS department. Apple, developers of the Macintosh, created a marketing program that was very close to a religious frenzy. (Their recent revival is also based on a marketing strategy where their customers "think differently" from the masses.)

The PC started a revolution in the development (and the cost of) software products. No longer was software development something confined to the mid-range and high-end systems. The personal computer provided a new

Smart things to say about e-commerce

Killer application

An incredibly useful creative program that provides a breakthrough for its users. The first killer app of the Internet was email.

entry point for developers of software, and the leaders in the business understood this trend. Bill Gates left Harvard University early to take advantage of the market opportunity. (Did rather well didn't he?) Steve Jobs identified another killer application, desktop publishing for the Macintosh, and Adobe and many software vendors headed for start-up capital and an expanding marketplace.

As all this was going on, the IT market became very polarized. Mid- and high-range vendors tried to ignore the PC and allowed new vendors to build their businesses at an incredible rate. As IBM and Intel left the door open from the architecture perspective (although IBM tried later to close it with OS/2 and the microchannel architecture) the market grew. New companies such as Dell, Compaq and Gateway forged a path in the marketplace, building PCs from this open architecture. All of this provided the foundation for the next level of market demand.

Organizations now had a collection of productive islands of computing, but needed to leverage them. The answer was to connect their machines to

Smart things to say about e-commerce

Local Area Network (LAN)

A computer network that operates and is located in one specific location. Many of these may be connected together in order to enable users to share resources and information on their network.

form a network. Banyan and Novell built entire companies around the networking of PCs and other machines. The world of workgroup computing and the Local Area Network was born. Initially the applications were simple. File sharing and printing provided the foundation of many of those early systems. However, with the entry level for software firms now lower than ever before, the opportunity to develop and distribute systems at a lower cost created hundreds of start-ups writing software for the PC.

The reason that this information is important to the evolution of the Internet is simple. The Internet is a network of computers, and it works in the same way as a Local Area Network, with a few differences. It has an industry standard protocol for communication between systems, and a common language to converse and present data between differing systems.

The information diagram illustrates how information networks are constructed. If an individual wants to communicate with these systems, they

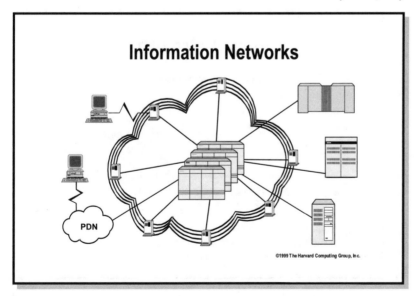

Information Networks

PDN

©1999 The Harvard Computing Group, Inc.

EXAMPLE OF PUBLIC AND PRIVATE NETWORKS	
Service	Private or Public
America OnLine	Private
MSN	Private
Internet	Public

require access to this Private Data Network. These networks are the basis of many computer operations around the world. You need to understand the differences between the private networks and the public one we call

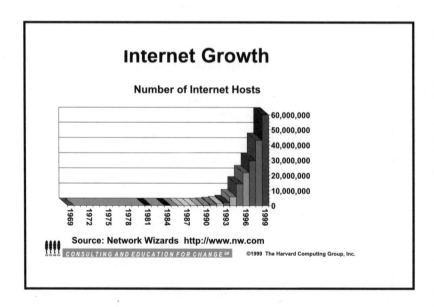

the Internet. Many large firms also manage their own private networks to meet their specific security and business requirements.

Of all networks, the Internet represents the largest collection of computers in the world today. The growth has been meteoric in recent years, but it took a while to get started. The chart above tells the story of adoption in recent years.

The components of the Internet world

In order to understand just how open and powerful the Internet has become, we need to review a few more details of its components.

Every computer on the Internet has it's own unique name. This is called a domain name, in addition to the domain name, each system has an exten-

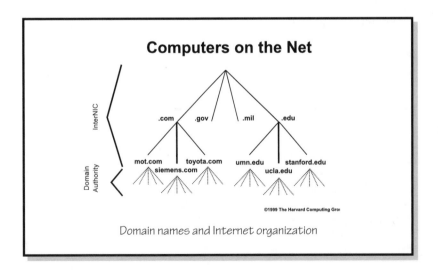

Domain names and Internet organization

Smart things
to say about
e-commerce

Domain name

The unique name that is used to identify a collection of Internet host computers. It contains two or more parts separated by a dot.

The most common domain names fit into one of six categories: educational institutions; commercial organizations; military; government; miscellaneous organizations; and networking organizations, e.g., ibm.com or whitehouse.gov

Geographic domain names end with a two-character country code, e.g., capstone.co.uk

sion. The extension usually describes the general function of the holder of the domain name.

Although there have recently been some changes in the use of extensions, they generally follow these principles. The .coms are usually companies or commercial operations, .nets are often Internet Service Providers, .mil is the military and so on.

For computers to talk to one another on the Internet, a valid domain name is required to make the connection. Each of these unique connections al-

Smart things
to say about
e-commerce

InterNIC

Governing body controlling the issuance and control of generic Internet domains and addresses. Currently a partnership between the US government and Network Solutions, Inc.

Geographic domain names are administered within each country connected to the Internet.

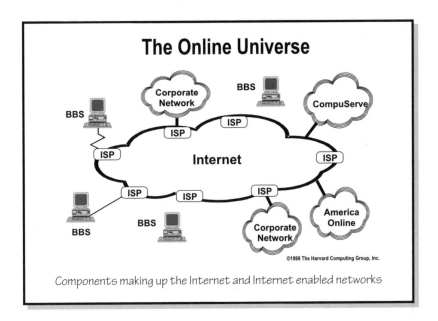

The Online Universe

Components making up the Internet and Internet enabled networks

lows us to ensure that we always connect to a valid member of the Internet, and that the members have become Internet citizens through a policing system known as the Internic. The Internic is the sole authority to issue domain names for companies, and ensures that each name is unique and managed independently through this process.

When we connect to the Internet, we connect to a network. In a typical workgroup organization this connection is usually a physical connection to a network in the office. We get around this problem with remote access by using dial up connections using a modem to connect to remote computers in the system. These computers then become part of the network.

There are many applications on the Internet, but the most common and frequently used ones are those in the following table. Even if you are not

LIST OF MAJOR APPLICATION PRODUCTS AND TOOLS FOR
INTERNET BASED APPLICATIONS

Application	Function	Product used
Electronic Mail	Interpersonal and world-wide communication of electronic messages and files	Any email enabled browser, or Internet compatible email client software
Browser applications for the WWW	Visit sites, or run web-based applications	Browser software from Microsoft, Netscape or others
Bulletin Board	Information sharing via specific databases that are public or private	Most bulletin boards are now accessible via web browsers
FTP (File transfer protocol)	Provides a way to upload and download data and software to and from Internet hosts. Can be public or private access	FTP transfer software programs
Newsgroups	Provide discussion groups that are useful for industry and professional information. Information is shared	Most browsers, support newsgroup functions directly
Chat and Instant messaging	Interactive (almost) discussion groups with members pre-selecting themselves	Netscape AOL Instant Messenger, Microsoft Instant Messenger, ICQ, Service specific chat rooms

Application	Function	Product used
Conferencing	Various means of communicating with others via the Internet, used for voice, video and data conferencing	Microsoft NetMeeting and many more on the market. Now often offered as part of a site service, with the hosting included
Communications and search tools	Telnet allows you to log into remote computers, Gopher is now built into most browsers today	Included with most browsers and transparent for users today
Mail list servers	Designed to allow bulk email delivery to a selected group of individuals	Offered by most Internet Services Providers as option. Can be purchased as software products

familiar with some of these applications it is very likely that someone in your organization is using some or all of these applications in support of your web site or internal applications. Over time, more of these applications are becoming available via a simple browser interface, avoiding the need for specialized software or interfaces.

Smart answers to tough questions

Q: What is the difference between the Internet and the world wide web?
A: The Internet is a collection of computers physically connected by a huge network and common communication protocols. The world wide web is one of a number of applications running across the computers on the Internet.

Smart things
to say about
e-commerce

Internet service provider (ISP)

Internet service providers sell connections to the Internet. Many ISPs also deliver a wide range of services to individual users and organizations including web site hosting, electronic mail, FTP, and e-commerce services.

Internet service providers and hosting companies

Companies known as Internet Service Providers (ISPs) sell access to the Internet as their primary product. They also supply electronic mail service, web page hosting, FTP access and the other applications. They deliver these services by combining lots of computing resources with high performance connections to the Internet in secure computing facilities known as data centers. These centers are often built to withstand significant natural weather disasters, have their own generators as back up, and are often "duplicated" in a huge network to provide failsafe data recovery in the event of a power failure or other catastrophe. The largest ISPs have huge membership roles, for example, America Online had 20 million subscribers as of November 1999.

While it is technically possible for any company to connect directly to the backbone of the Internet, most companies choose an Internet service provider to support their Internet access for a variety of reasons:

- it's cheaper;

- they do not have to deal with security or firewall issues internally;

- it reduces system maintenance;

- the ISP screens junk mail;

- the ISP hosts domain names that meet specific company requirements; and

- the ISP provides support for the company's Internet users.

In the early years of Internet connectivity, leading companies wanting to be on the Internet hosted their own systems internally and purchased Internet access and dedicated bandwidth from a Telecom firm offering these services.

In early 1995, the market started to change. Many more firms and individuals wanted to access the Internet and to establish a presence on the World Wide Web, but did not have the knowledge, capital or desire to do it themselves. (Setting up your own system in-house requires significant knowledge about security and firewall systems to avoid external unauthorized access to internal computer systems.)

Consequently, two types of services emerged in the marketplace. Some service providers primarily focused on individual users who needed to browse the Internet and have access to on-line information services. A second group of firms focused on providing e-mail, web hosting, ftp and other services to small and medium size businesses. The second group of service providers allowed firms to establish a web presence, have relatively high speed access (better than dial-up services), but not have to install dedicated software and computer systems to host their web sites, or manage their Internet e-mail. Service Providers such as America Online,

---

Hosting service

Company that hosts your web site at their facilities, offering high reliability and bandwidth along with redundancy, security and other services.

Smart things to say about e-commerce

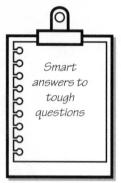

Smart
answers to
tough
questions

Q: When should I consider a company specific site with my own domain name versus those provided by my ISP with their web address?

A: As soon as you have a need to "brand" your own organization or company site. This way you have your own identity and greater control over the content and the experience that your visitors will encounter.

CompuServe, Prodigy and MSN grew quickly and a "marketing war" broke out over users and their service fees. Today there are more than 4,000 Internet Service Providers in the United States alone, so the market remains very competitive and the range of services offered changes frequently.

One decision many of you will have to make early in your e-commerce strategy is how much of the operation of your e-commerce site is going to be brought in-house. In some cases, where security is critical, there are few choices. We do not expect banks or financial trading institutions to outsource the hosting of their systems anytime soon. However, many other businesses are outsourcing many of their important Internet based information systems, and we expect this trend to continue.

In 1997 and 1998 another breed of firm entered the market. These dedicated, high-end hosting companies provided some of the same services as the traditional ISPs, but with a twist. They focused on mission critical applications that needed significant network bandwidth and reliability –

Smart things to say about e-commerce

Application service provider

Hosting service that will operate, support, manage and maintain your application with staff for a fee.

the sort that could previously only be obtained by individual companies setting up their own data centers and backup systems. These companies particularly targeted voice and video applications that require huge network and computing resources. Now with the appropriate infrastructure in place, many have become very successful.

Some hosting companies are now moving towards a new market space, that of the application service provider (ASP). In this scenario, the service provider hosts your traditional and web applications, i.e. applications like ERP, accounting and even desktop productivity software, on their computer systems, and provides full support and maintenance. In addition, some offer back up and high performance features such as mirroring, replication and on-demand bandwidth increases at peak times. Some application service providers also offer e-commerce features as part of hosting offerings for companies of all sizes.

The serious user will often opt to use a dedicated hosting provider. These companies provide the facilities that you would otherwise have to build for yourself, but share the cost of the facilities and support among their customers. Many companies like this option as it can save up-front costs for the Internet connection and reduce maintenance costs over the life of the system. Companies such as Digex, Exodus, and NaviSite are fast growing specialists in this sector of the market.

Intranets and extranets

The tools of the Internet are not just for external use. It is relatively easy for us to take the architecture of the "big" Internet and scale it for use in our own environments. The following list of items will allow you to create your own "internal Internet":

- a TCIP/IP network

- electronic mail server

- email client software

- web server

- a browser or client software application

- chat

- FTP.

With this shopping list you now have all the advantages of the Internet but have customized the technology to your own internal requirements.

Intranets have incredible advantages over existing forms of groupware and office communication systems. These include:

- browser based (everyone can be a user)

- people friendly

- easier to develop (than previous generation systems)

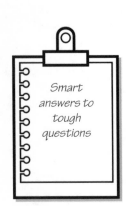

Smart
answers to
tough
questions

Q: What is an intranet?
A: An Intranet is an Internet network that is located inside the organization, and not generally accessible by the general public. It is based on the same technology components as the Internet.

- easy to change

- lower cost than traditional development alternatives

- very high payback

- based on standards that everyone should support

- easier to update

- easily customized

- perform well

- scale better than most applications.

The development of an intranet has become a major component of many organizations' e-business strategies. Intranet systems evolve from many starting points. These run the gamut from strategic initiatives with enterprise support, to others developed at the departmental level and some that have been opportunistic based on speed and cost constraints. Whatever the reasons, intranets have established themselves at the core of many IT strategies. Even organizations that have resisted the gravitational pull of the technology are adopting intranet strategies.

In the beginning, intranets were either located in data centers or out in the departments. In recent years, the number of intranets within organizations has grown dramatically. This has created a need to integrate content, maintain performance, share information, control access and deal with intranets in differing locations. Multiple intranet servers, connected by local and wide area networks, provide the foundation for distributed intranets.

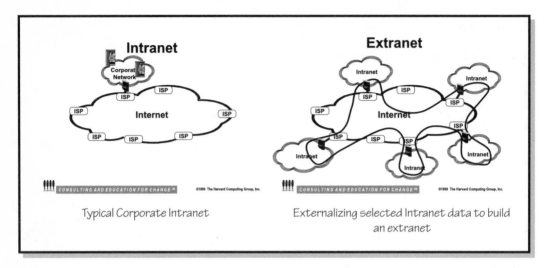

Typical Corporate Intranet   Externalizing selected Intranet data to build an extranet

Today, most organizations have moved from the view that intranets are a separate component of their IT strategy. Intranets are a flexible way of organizing information where the content can be shared with others in a controlled and expandable way. This philosophy provides the foundation for the development of distributed intranets. Also as intranets become richer in content, and this content is extended to partners and customers, more extranets are born. From the architectural point of view, an extranet is merely a protected section of an intranet.

Many firms develop intranets to improve productivity and increase the speed with which information is delivered inside their organizations. In environments that have a great need to provide accurate information in more timely and distributed ways, the intranet and its natural ability to expand has made it the technology choice of many.

This evolution is not limited to *pure* intranet solutions; it also includes groupware as office and workgroup applications becoming Internet en-

Application	Intranet	Extranet
TABLE ILLUSTRATING INTRANET APPLICATIONS AND ACCESS CHARACTERISTICS		
Employee telephone directory	Yes	Selected contact listing
HR policies	Yes	No
Support information	Yes	Yes, but controlled access
Knowledge Base	Yes	Selected components on password protected basis

abled. These solutions are becoming more intranet-based, with browser-based Interfaces, compatible with web servers and supportive of web standards. However, the underlying databases and data structures vary according to application and platform focus.

The extranet therefore becomes the external part of your Internet strategy, the part of your system that you want to communicate with your business partners and clients. Smart companies can achieve dramatic reduction of timeframes and costs with a careful combination of Internet, intranet and extranet programs. We will cover later the ingredients that you need to make all this work.

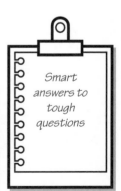

Smart answers to tough questions

Q: What is the difference between an intranet and an extranet?
A: Intranets facilitate sharing of information by people in a single organization. Extranets facilitate sharing of information by individuals in multiple organizations and are the result of business partners connecting portions of their intranets to meet common business goals.

How web software works

Host-based applications and client/server LAN applications typically require unique desktop software for every application. One of the most dramatic advantages of web-based applications is that the desktop software is always the same. (Well, almost always. Security applications may require more complex software that we will look at in later chapters.) Your users only require a web browser to view millions of web pages or to interact with web-based applications.

A request from a web browser to a web server and the corresponding response take place using a language known as HTML (hypertext markup language). Before the invention of HTML and the world wide web, the

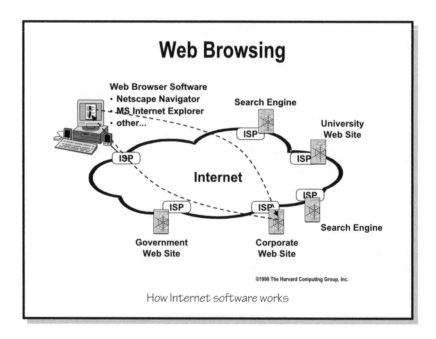

How Internet software works

While working at Cern, the European particle physics laboratory, in Geneva, Switzerland, Berners-Lee created the world wide web. He is known as the father of the world wide web.

SMART PEOPLE
TO HAVE ON
YOUR SIDE:

TIM
BERNERS-LEE

idea of public access to so many software systems and computers with a single piece of software would have been considered unbelievable. The browser has changed our lives.

As we develop and deploy Internet technology, we often hear about differing types of architecture, and how one is superior to the other. In general, there are two types of software firms in the market, ones that have developed their software specifically for the Internet and others that are changing their software to catch up with the others. Do not worry about any other software firms for your e-commerce strategy. You only want to do business with companies that have an effective web strategy.

Software categorization for the web can be very confusing for both novices and experts. Much of the confusion is caused by the sheer rate of change in the marketplace, combined with a lot of vapor flying around in vendor marketing materials. (Later in the book, we will spend more time on the subject of selecting software vendors and partners.)

Technology food groups

The basic food groups that will influence our technology decisions on the web are categorized below.

Smart
answers to
tough
questions

Q: What is a horizontal application?
A: Applications such as electronic mail, bulletin boards and chat systems are horizontal applications. These are ready to run, without much need for customization and can be used for many different internal or business-to-business communication needs. They can be used to support many vertical or industry specific functions.

1 *Horizontal applications*

Most of the earlier applications and tools mentioned fit into this group. Electronic Mail, newsgroups and bulletin boards are all examples of horizontal applications. Today, most of these have reached a commodity pricing level, and are included in other applications for a small fee. Increasingly they are being offered free.

2 *Packaged applications*

Turnkey applications that perform a particular application without major modification are becoming available for the Internet. Customer management applications, document management systems, project management systems all fall into this category. Previously these applications were typically developed for client/server applications for a local area, or wide area network.

3 *Web servers*

The web server is at the heart of any web-based application. The server receives requests from web browsers or other applications, interfaces with database systems, manages interactions with other servers or applications, and formats and delivers responses.

4   *Database systems and application servers*

Database products store, manipulate and provide the information to send to web servers. They are the brains of the system, storing the most valuable information and processing trades and transactions.

5   *Security systems*

Your security system is the most important aspect of your e-commerce solution. Without security you do not have a system, you have a liability. Security typically is defined for computers, networks, users, applications and even down to specific transactions.

6   *Tools and other systems*

You will use a myriad of other tools in the development of your e-commerce system, ranging from authoring, maintenance, administration and optimization to marketing and others. We will discuss these areas in more detail in Chapter 2.

Portals

A portal is a destination site for users of a particular class. In the past we have defined a portal as any site with a large number of visitors on which the primary focus was not to sell product. However, many large portals are becoming full service e-commerce sites and many e-commerce sites are attempting to position themselves as portals. Despite the blurring of this line, most individuals see the portal as a non-commercial Internet site, providing information or entertainment for them during their visit. The

> **Portal**
>
> Major visiting center for Internet users. The very large portals started life as search engines, AltaVista, AOL, CompuServe, Excite, Infoseek, Lycos, Magellan, and Yahoo are examples of major portals.

large portals have evolved primarily from the search engines sites and include AOL, Yahoo, Excite, Northern Light, Lycos and Netscape.

The portal market is changing. As web users get smarter, they will migrate to sites that can offer a more complete and relevant experience for them. In the business world, we have seen the birth of another form of portal, the Corporate Information Portal. This allows users to interact with information and systems relevant to the corporate world, and is customizable to meet their needs.

At the application end of the business, new portals are being defined based on the use of a "free" service on the web, such as email or calendaring. In response to this specialized competition, the major portals such as Yahoo and Lycos are adding similar capabilities on a regular basis.

There is no question that the portal marketplace is changing daily. As more companies with a presence on the Internet understand that content is one of the most important issues that continues to bring visitors back to their site, these categories of web sites can do nothing but increase. The vertical portal, focused on an industry group is now one of the fastest growing sectors of the marketplace. If you want to stay abreast of activities in your industry, watch this space carefully. The vertical portals will ultimately change the way that business is done, particularly for partnership creation and business networking.

Corporate Information portal
(corechange.com)

Vertical portal
(brint.com)

International portal
(yahoo.com)

National portal
(china.com)

Regional portal
(boston.com)

Search portal
(altavista.com)

Examples of portals currently offering mixture of services to visitors

Integrators and strategy development partners

Unless we have unlimited resources in our organizations, it is likely that we will have to consider using some form of external help to deploy our e-commerce systems. Consequently, the decisions we make in selecting integrators and development partners are crucial to the success of our e-commerce projects. The wrong choice will cause us many problems, while the right one could result in a dramatic expansion of our operation.

Our choice of integrators and development partners will be based on our assessment of our internal capabilities. After evaluating our strengths and weaknesses, the following are likely areas in which to request help:

- strategy development

- market research

- application specification and project management

- development and coding

- quality assurance and testing

- roll-out and training.

Many integrators offer a full range of services to assist businesses of varying sizes with their e-commerce systems. It is likely that you are already being bombarded with invitations to seminars for e-commerce strategy or product offerings to improve the way that your business is operating. When selecting partners, we must first understand how we are going to use them in order to make the best decisions.

TYPES OF DEVELOPMENT AND CONSULTING COMPANIES
IN THE E-COMMERCE SPACE

Project needs	Type of consulting firms	What to look for
Strategy consulting	e-commerce strategy development firms, management consulting firms specializing in e-commerce area	Track record of development of strategy through to the implementation of systems and company roll out
Research for e-commerce marketplace	Research firms specializing in e-commerce marketplace	Specialized research capabilities to ensure that your target market is being addressed. Target marketing skills with good results for their client base
Application specification and project management	E-commerce strategy development firms, management consulting firms specializing in e-commerce	Good project management skills, excellent facilitation and new work process skills. Most e-commerce systems require great change to occur in work process and practices
Development and coding, quality assurance and testing, roll-out and training	Development firms specializing in e-commerce marketplace	Strong development skills in e-commerce technology in your industry or technology area. High quality resources with good skills in high demand new relevant skills

There is such a significant demand for e-commerce development assistance that there is a severe shortage of developers and project managers with the right experience. The firms that are experienced and have many references are very backlogged, difficult to schedule and more expensive than firms with less experience. However, we don't want to become the learning curve for developers that do not yet have a track record of developing e-commerce systems. At the end of the day, we hire consultants to reduce risk and improve the potential for good outcomes so this is not a time to pick the wrong firm.

We can categorize integration firms into several groups for e-commerce development, each having benefits, strengths and weaknesses for different types of work. The preceding table provides some guidelines for different types of assistance, with examples of firms in each category.

As we embark on the e-commerce road, we must consider the various elements and waypoints along the journey. There are many variables in this marketplace, and a continuously changing landscape. The trip will be exciting.

Picking partners is however, only one part of the process. First, we need to take a deep breath and ready ourselves for the big one. Change.

2
Think E-commerce – Think Change!

Think e-commerce, think change. Change, and your appetite for change often determine the level of success in the first implementation of an e-commerce strategy. Leading companies have created dramatic value with their e-commerce initiatives and continue to be successful. We can consider e-commerce as:

- a strategy

- a technology

- a system

- a separate business

- a sales approach

Smart things
to say about
e-commerce

E-commerce spending

For every dollar spent on business-to-consumer e-commerce, business-to-business e-commerce spends five more. (This gap is expected to stretch to 10 times over the next five years according to Forrester Research.)

- a mystery or

- some combination of the above.

Most of the media focus on e-commerce has kept us focused on the business-to-consumer marketplace, buying products via the web. This has in fact obscured our attention of what has become the larger part of this evolving marketplace, business to business e-commerce solutions.

Preparing for change

In order to prepare ourselves for this type of change, we have to be ready to modify our behavior in a big way. Many organizations prepare themselves to make these changes in several ways.

Today we hear much about Internet time. Preparing ourselves to compete and make decisions in Internet time can be a frightening proposition. Par-

Smart things
to say about
e-commerce

Internet time

Internet time is a common expression of how fast the Internet world can change. Internet years are generally measured on a scale of 60 days for one traditional calendar year.

Smart answers to tough questions

Q: How do I evaluate risk in determining my e-commerce?
A: Imagine that you are working for your most feared competitor, that they have twice as much money to spend and can implement your e-commerce strategy in six months. Then decide how much risk is reasonable.

ticularly since we may not be comfortable enough with the outcome to predict some level of success. However, there is a need to ensure that some level of risk is considered OK to move forward.

One way of getting ready for a different method of operation is to arm ourselves with the right information. However, this is only part of the process. We also have to consider how we are going to determine what level of risk is acceptable and what level is dangerous.

A useful method to prepare for this change is to look at your own individual marketplace and determine whether you are going to be a leader, follower or a victim. There are two potential outcomes that allow a company or organization to be successful, the latter has a somewhat darker end.

In e-commerce, doing nothing has outcomes just like any other strategy. If the market is in the early stages it is possible that we can do nothing and avoid wasting resources and finances. However, the leader who took the

Moore's Law

Intel founder Gordon Moore predicted that the performance (and chip density) of computers would double every 18 months while the price would remain the same.

Smart things to say about e-commerce

Smart things
to say about
e-commerce

Metcalf's Law

Robert Metcalf, founder of 3COM, predicted that the value of a network will dramatically increase as every new node is added to the network.

chance and did it anyway may have failed, but they also learned something in the process. They also are likely to have gained some specific skills in marketing, technology, support and organization change that will make it easier next time. Therefore, sometimes failing can cause you to win in the end.

Smart people know how important it is to prepare for these changes in mindset. One of the best methods of understanding the risk and reward is to look at how others have dealt with change.

The technology influence

Even if we decide to do nothing, the environment around us is going to change anyway. One driving force in this change is technology.

Moore's Law and, more recently, Metcalfe's Law are often quoted in the media to explain these factors. Moore's Law, which has proven to be true for more than 30 years, has made computing technology increasingly af-

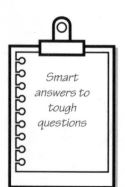

Smart
answers to
tough
questions

Q: What two technology factors impact the adoption of e-commerce systems?
A: The systems are becoming more and more affordable, and the user base of customers is increasing dramatically over time.

E-commerce offers

- large numbers of potential users
- ability to publish new information on demand
- increasing ability to deliver product directly to the end user
- customization capabilities to target the product directly to the needs of the end user
- electronic software distribution (to deliver the solution).

fordable. However, it is Metcalfe's Law, the law of connected computing that influences the e-commerce space for all of us. The combination of these two has produced a distributed computing world of customers with browsers at the ready.

Few, if any, of us have ever been faced with a potential market of millions, all of whom are connected to the same channel, providing us with an affordable method of communication to almost any target audience. We have to rethink everything about our approach to the market.

Smart quotes

You have to look where the puck is going to be, not where it is now.

Wayne Gretzky (Hall of Fame Hockey Player)

Although technology never makes a marketplace on its own, it has provided the vehicle. Internet technology is available almost everywhere on the planet, allowing products and services to be offered on a scale never possible before. Just consider how research was done before the Internet. Some schools in the United States will currently not let kids submit their research based on what they have found on the Internet. Why? Because they want kids to learn how to do traditional research from trusted sources, to understand how to use a library and other published materials to reach conclusions. We have come to expect instant results and conclusions.

With such a large amount of data available, finding the relevant information can be the challenge for most of us. But wait for it, there are products coming onto the market specifically to address this issue.

Smart quotes

The network is the computer.

Sun Microsystems advertisement from the 1980s

How to compete in a free *market*

As the Internet has developed, we have moved through several evolving business models. However, just as we have become familiar with one model, another changes or challenges the principle. We can expect this changing landscape to continue for the foreseeable future.

One aspect of this is what is free and what we pay for on the Internet. The table opposite illustrates how businesses are offering services for increasingly powerful and complex applications, but instead of raising the price for increased services, firms are giving them away.

As the table below illustrates, it is difficult to see how (or sometimes why) anyone is going to make any money on the Internet. Do not be fooled by this. Many of the sites and companies that are subsidizing these free services are doing it for several good reasons.

Why companies are giving away services on the Internet

- We can make money from advertising by giving away useful services and information.

- We are willing to lose money while we create a community.

- We are creating a community that will drive business and target clients to our site offering other services.

EXAMPLES OF HOW INTERNET COSTS ARE CHANGING

Service	Initially	Currently (1999)	In the future
Searching	Free	Free	Free
Electronic mail	Subscription	Subscription and Free	Free
Bulletin boards	Subscription	Subscription and Free	Free
Newsgroups	Free	Free	Free
Instant messaging	Subscription	Subscription and Free	Free
Individual hosting services	Subscription	Subscription and Free	Free
Extranet services	Software based fee	Subscription and software fee	Free, subscription and software fee
Mail list servers	Software based fee, subscription service	Subscription service (some software products)	Free and subscription
Web hosting	Subscription based	Subscription and free	Subscription and free

- We can make money by referring others to our site.

- We want to control the world.

Aside from the last reason, there is method in the madness of giving things away on the Internet.

Traditional entry to the market could be harmful to your health

So smart people know that considering only traditional approaches could be the very thing that causes an e-commerce strategy to fail before you have even started.

In the early stages of many companies' strategies on the web, there is a rush to put up what was called a "vanity site" or "brochureware". Many substantial companies still have sites that reflect this approach. The sites are static and not well maintained. Many even have spelling mistakes and old addresses. For any company wanting to present a reasonable image to their clients, this is the equivalent of unpleasing graffiti all over the walls of your headquarters. Unacceptable.

Leave tradition for weddings and funerals. It will not do us any good on the web. Understanding how to develop innovative approaches without great risk is the mark of many successes in this industry. But don't expect it to be cheap. Despite what you may have heard, building (and promoting) a good web site is not cheap. I do not care how good your 13-year-old kid is with the latest web tool, they will not be able to represent your corporation as well as a firm that knows how to translate your goals into a finished system. You may get what you paid for, a cheap job.

Smart things to say about e-commerce

Brochureware

The act of putting your corporate literature in basic static form directly to a web site. Often bores visitors to death, and causes rapid exits from the site.

Q: What are the smart questions to ask yourself before starting an e-commerce development?

A: - How many visitors would you like have at your site?
- What message do you want them to get?
- Do you want to build a community?
- Is the site a transaction site?
- Are there customer support requirements?

Acclimatizing yourself and others in the organization to this type of thinking is a good warm up to the real development of the strategy.

Smart answers to tough questions

Companies and organizations must consider the objectives for their site before starting. We cannot just replicate the corporate literature and expect it to be a winner.

Change thinking

The critical first step is to identify the objectives for our e-commerce site. Then we can use these goals as the vehicle for initiating change in our approach to the marketplace.

SAMPLE BUSINESS GOALS AND E-COMMERCE GOALS

Business goals	E-commerce goals
Provide on-line customer support function	Create customer support database that will fulfill 60% of current help desk calls
Sell products on-line	Build secure e-commerce facility for existing and new clients
Create community of interested prospects	Develop "vertical interest" to provide visitors with a reason to visit and return

> **Smart things to say about e-commerce**

> We need to:
>
> • provide on-line customer support function;
> • sell products on-line; and
> • create community of interested prospects.

A process of new strategy development needs a different mindset to consider how to develop and implement the system. If you create a clear set of business goals and then transfer them to objectives for the e-commerce strategy, you will reduce risk from the business strategy.

Competition – it may be closer than you think

We often consider competition as one of the last reasons for change and e-commerce (unless you have left it really late in your market space). Competitors can use the Internet as an unfair advantage against you, and this is in fact a smart way to look at developing e-commerce systems. Leveraging what you already have in place can make a dramatic difference in the way that you bring your strategy into place.

For example, consider two medium-size furniture companies that are both looking to put e-commerce systems in place for their distributors.

Company A decides to take an aggressive approach, knowing that Company B does not have a serious web presence. They want to get there first, and hire a local web designer to come and "get them up and running in 30 days or less."

The process looks like this:

- Web designer A reviews company A and its brochures.

- Designer provides a boiler plate site framework, with the usual About Us, Message from the President, Mission and a nice walk through of their furniture line with descriptions and sample pictures.

- Company A approves the new site.

They are up and running on the web in advance of their competition. Goal achieved.

Company B takes a different approach. Company B looks at their overall business goals. These include reducing inventory turns, increasing sales, and gaining better performance from its distribution network.

> Smart things
> to say about e-commerce
>
> When developing your strategy, look for high value and high impact changes that will generate big returns for you, your clients and shareholders.

Company B conducts an internal review of these goals and determines that there are some serious problems with their distribution channel and loyalty with their dealers. Then they hire a firm to determine the business and technical requirements of their new system.

This process produces a realization that:

- More loyalty and customer satisfaction could be achieved by allowing business partners to place orders and get delivery dates for orders via a controlled extranet application.

- By designing an e-commerce system to integrate with existing manufacturing and inventory management system, their partners can gain access to this information easily.

- Because of this service, customers visiting their distributors' stores are offered almost instant information about delivery schedules (company A's clients have to wait until the store is open on Monday, and get a telephone call response, well after their client has left the store while shopping at the weekend).

- It can develop a web site that has a theme for different types of decorating tastes and styles and it can organize the site so clients can view the furniture by manufacturer, style or taste.

- A search capability could be added to the site to allow distributors and their customers to find furniture based on style.

Although company B came to market later with their solution, the results they achieved were much more significant. They thought through how they were going to use the technology to help achieve their business goals. (A surprising number of firms still do the technology first, and then hope it will do something for the business.) They also used a firm that could translate their business goals into a system that would give them a sustainable competitive advantage versus their competitors. The other firm's clients still have to make a telephone call before they can determine availability of the product their client needs.

Smart things to say about e-commerce

Leverage your existing technology and systems to improve customer service and support improved sales cycles.

Second guessing your competitors

Another good strategy to use in warming up for e-commerce change is to play the following scenario.

1. You define your new product strategy for e-commerce.

2. You then launch the product.

3. Then your competition comes out with a revised or more competitive offering to your new product.

What do you do? The answer is of course to consider the reaction before you launch the product. This way you will examine how others may counter your strategy before it comes to market, therefore allowing you to review either the existing plan, or be ready with some alternative changes as they come to the marketplace. Many firms do not consider this scenario in the marketplace, and then are sideswiped by the competition.

Traditional marketing strategies don't always work

In the world of traditional markets we have a set of reference points that do not always do us favors. Many software (and other) companies that are focusing on the Internet exclusively have developed their strategies by being very contrary to traditional business thinking. Some of the leading firms on the Internet today were started on a shoestring. Their common link was that they wanted to create a "community" of users, and provide a valuable experience at their sites (e.g. Yahoo). Others have spent vast amounts of money to create huge user communities or to develop a "brand" at any cost. (Amazon.com, America Online).

Traditional marketing strategies can cause the effect shown in the table overleaf.

Out of the box thinking is often referred to as a method of ensuring that you do not limit the potential alternatives for your e-commerce system. That does not mean that you have to do seek and destroy missions through-out the organization, causing chaos and consternation everywhere.

TRADITIONAL STRATEGIES CAN ENFORCE LIMITED RESULTS	
Traditional strategy	Potential outcome
Stick to existing business model and try and replicate it on the web	Does not provide significant improvement in sales, service or customer satisfaction
Sell the existing product on the web	May be more opportunities to offer broader range of product on the web
Protect my existing distribution strategy	Some of the current distribution channels may not be adding enough value to warrant protection. May leave money on the table
Limit impact on internal operations	Minimizes the opportunity for productivity improvements

Nevertheless, smart people know that existing processes and situations can be improved dramatically.

To avoid some of these problems, and start the juices going, just consider the way that traditional decision making can result in the wrong type of change happening in the organization.

Smart quotes

Comfort is not the objective in a visionary company. Indeed, visionary companies install powerful mechanisms to create *dis*comfort-to obliterate complacency-and thereby stimulate change and improvement *before* the external world demands it.

James C. Collins and Jerry I. Porras, *Built to Last*

Smart things to say about e-commerce

> About IT projects:
>
> - 45% of IT projects are late or over budget;
> - nearly 30% arere abandoned, scaled back or modified;
> - only about 25% arere completed on time and on budget.
>
> Source: a study of 7500 IT projects conducted by Standish Group International (1998)

Avoiding bad decisions

All too often, we only ask questions like these at the end of yet another ruined project. A recent study of 7500 IT projects conducted by Standish Group International in 1998 the results given in the box above.

Amazingly, we do not appear to be learning from our mistakes in technology selection, although the systems, software and implementation methodologies are more mature than ever before. Consolidation in industry, richer application development platforms and rapid application development tools should all lead us to greater implementation success. Why are failure rates so high? Here are some of the reasons why things go wrong.

Scenario one – the candy store

Many technology buys are just this, technology purchases. Users and management become like kids in the veritable candy store. Thousands of dollars are spent buying generic research and visiting trade shows in an effort to become an expert on what is available in the marketplace. Don't make the mistake of spending too little time understanding how it will affect your business.

Scenario two – the crusade syndrome

Once enamored with a technology, there is usually no stopping the crusader. The battle cry becomes, "Now that I understand what's out there and know that I need one, all I have to do is convince all the others why they should have one too." Unfortunately, the outcome is often all too similar to the original crusades – lots of bloodshed and not as many converts as you would like.

Scenario three – death by analysis

Analyze the problem to death and then specify the system needs. You cannot be wrong. Every possible requirement has been identified through a series of very expensive interviews and collated using a database or methodology ideally suited to the process. Every need has been homogenized, pasteurized, analyzed, qualified and prioritized. Now we have the "corporate view" encapsulated in a statistical representation of the whole organization's needs, but we have so much detail that nothing is clear. The technology has also probably changed while all this was going on.

Scenario four – do it now, and do it fast!

Often following one of the above, particularly when it has taken too long, management issues an edict. The team is forced into action. Without a game plan, they are forced to react. Emergency decisions produce emergency results, which are seldom satisfactory.

We get what we deserve

Buying technology without understanding our business goals and how we are going to use it is a recipe for failure. (Who has not been responsible for a "shelfware" decision in their organization at some time?) If you buy a product and merely hope that people will use it, you will not succeed. Chapter 6 will deal with specific strategies to avoid any of the above problems.

Factor in the culture element

Another factor that influences our ability to change things in the organization is the cultural element. Creating the right environment for the adoption of the e-commerce system, and rewarding staff accordingly can make the difference between success and failure. Many organizations assume

---

CULTURE AND WORK PRACTICE ISSUES THAT AFFECT DEPLOYMENT AND SUCCESS OF E-COMMERCE SYSTEMS

Example of culture	Result
Tremendous reward to individual efforts	More resistance to teambuilding and team rewarding initiatives
Entrapped in current work practices	Resistance to change
Hierarchical management	Difficult to adjust to collaborative team model
Driven by common corporate and employee goals/rewards	Rapidly adopt technology to support business and workgroup functions
Technology driven	Needs help to assist with workgroup productivity and process issues
Technophobic	Needs significant persuasion to use technology at all

---

that traditional individual reward schemes will provide the incentive for change, but there are other issues that can cause the culture to reject the system.

Failure to understand and address these issues will ultimately influence the organization's achievements. Many e-commerce productivity gains are based on effective behavior change in the enterprise; therefore it is critical to ensure that we link cultural and process change to the system. We can dramatically improve the potential for success by understanding these issues.

Identifying candidates for change

The chart opposite illustrates the importance of the relationships between the technology selection and the work practices inside the organization. Smart people will consider these relationships in their search for e-commerce candidate applications. Because we can easily deploy e-commerce technology to every desktop in the enterprise, consider the impact as information starts to be distributed directly to the staff that need it. Even this simple change in the publishing and availability of information can cause consternation in an operation that has been used to a hierarchical management structure, with "trickle down" information flows.

Looking for potential candidates for change is not as hard as you might think. Every business or organization has some areas that need improvement. Here are a few starting points to consider for e-commerce change.

Industry trends and innovations

Industries are changing the way that they use e-commerce as a lever. We

EXAMPLES OF E-COMMERCE TECHNOLOGY INFLUENCE INSIDE THE ORGANIZATION

Technology		Work Process and practices	
Before	After	Before	After
Departmental	Enterprise	Hierarchical	Across enterprise
Electronic publishing	Web publishing	Structured around release dates	Dynamic around change and organization needs
Application specific	Business function or organization specific	Information not easily re-purposed	Information re-purposed based on business needs
Client/server	Thin client	Not easily accessible from any point in organization	Easily accessible from any point in organization

© 1999 Harvard Computing Group, Inc.

must focus on the fundamental opportunities reviewed earlier in order to achieve great changes. The market is at an early stage of development, but there are still some good pointers to consider for each market sector. There

Smart things to say about e-commerce

Areas of the business to consider change:

- sales distribution strategies and support
- improvements in customer support systems
- changes in the distribution system
- creating new products and services
- sales and distribution changes.

is barely an industry today that has not been touched by the e-commerce bug. Each of us must determine how this change will affect us by looking at what industries and organizations like our own are doing. We all have to determine how and where best to affect this change.

Manufacturing and electronics

The manufacturing industry has produced incredible results using e-commerce systems in a very short period. Supply chain, procurement, customer management systems, knowledge management, and direct sales are but a few of the programs that are in operation. Many firms are using the Internet as a vehicle to broaden their distribution, supply chains and reach a global marketplace.

Pharmaceutical and biotech

Development and manufacturing of drugs is an expensive business. Exclusive manufacturing rights for new drugs are limited to a fixed number of years, so companies must get to market quickly. For many years these firms have understood the value of leveraging knowledge and using electronic workgroup technology to speed the research, discovery, development and approval cycles for their operations. E-commerce technologies can further improve manufacturing processes, along with development of sophisticated distribution programs directly to the pharmacy.

Smart things to say about e-commerce

E-tailing:

Online sales of retail style goods. Many consumer and specialist goods are now available via these on-line e-tailers.

Software

This industry is a natural for e-commerce. Software firms are embracing e-commerce by using knowledge bases to communicate with their business partners and customers, by delivering software downloads and fixes electronically, and by using superb tools to leverage their distribution channels.

Healthcare

Healthcare is using the Internet in some very interesting ways. At the physician level, videoconferencing, data conferencing and on-line patient records are allowing collaboration across long distances. On-line pharmacies are opening on a regular basis and content rich sites are building new networks in this market.

Retail

The retail market is growing, and the cost of entry is now so low that the smallest business can afford to get into the game. On-line shopping, complete with taxation and shipping software make it simple to get started. With many more shoppers on-line the growth is sure to continue.

Telecommunications

Most of the telecommunications applications to date are in the knowledge management and information transfer category. Companies that are global in this space need to transfer information, software and manage large projects across wide area networks. They also are using data marts and Internet technology to get closer to the consumer and market their services in an aggressive marketplace.

Utilities

Utility firms around the globe are facing change. Many countries have begun the process of deregulation. This means that utilities will be faced with competition in different sectors of their business operation. They will also have to undergo significant change as they move to a competitive commercial environment. E-commerce technology can help everywhere from maintenance, safety, sales, marketing and support of their systems.

Architecture, engineering and construction

Project management, collaboration and integration of services all would benefit from the use of e-commerce in an industry that continues to expand with the global economy. E-commerce will add a very significant collaboration tool to an industry that already uses technology for the design and support of its products and services.

Legal

The legal industry has been an electronic consumer for some time, primarily in the research zone. The Internet gives attorneys the ability to market themselves worldwide, and expand their presence and co-operation significantly. Case management across the Internet will allow firms to collaborate more effectively.

Government

Governments are committing to the Internet in a big way. Governments publish massive amounts of information and just the savings in distributing information are enormous. Many governments are also trying to improve their internal efficiency and operation. E-commerce is helping with this change.

SMART THINGS TO CONSIDER ABOUT E-COMMERCE AND CHANGE

- technology factors
- industry issues
- internal culture
- marketing strategy
- competition.

SMART VOICES

Entertainment

Video, film, music and multi-media are now a major part of the Internet. As the quality of service (QoS) increases and prices for high-speed connections drop, there will be tremendous opportunities for expansion in this sector of the market.

Finance, banking and insurance

Despite a slow start, on-line banking, insurance and financial services are here to stay. In some cases, they are forcing others to change the way they operate. (Several firms have now decided to offer out of hours trading on the New York Stock Exchange, as some leading firms have already blazed a trail). Many firms now want to offer a wide range of services to secure the attention of the consumers' finances, not just for banking, but also insurance, savings, retirement and estate planning.

Integrating the elements of change

With so many different angles to the issue of change even the smartest of you may be wondering where to start. Being ready for change and understanding why it is going to happen to your industry is really the most important element.

Despite the complex nature of these issues, you probably have a good handle on many of these already. Integrating the other factors in the development of your strategy will help you reduce risk and start to embrace change as a friend and not a foe.

There is no shortage of opportunities out there for us to pursue. We just have to think e-commerce, think "change!"

3

E-commerce Technologies that Matter

OK, so you thought that you got away with the technology part. Sorry. This is the technology chapter. Reading this section will not make you a expert in e-commerce technology, but it will stop you from being fooled with gobbledygook. Although the technology components are broad, the function they perform individually is not that tough to understand. This chapter will help you understand which pieces do what, and how best you can apply them in your organization.

The first thing to appreciate is that no vendor has it all. Maybe IBM could provide you with more than most, but in the main, you will be dealing with different products from different vendors and suppliers.

Some basic questions can help you lay some of the technology foundations for the system. These questions will start to provide the answers to the more complex issues of information delivery, security and Intranets and Extranet systems.

If you can answer some of the questions on the left, the technology components and direction will become more obvious.

KILLER QUESTIONS

- What are you going to sell?
- How are you going to sell it?
- How will it be delivered?
- Are you going to sell through partners?

Security

While security is a broad based subject, it can be broken down into different functions based on the way that you plan to manage your business partners and customers. Although some of these systems are very complex to understand and implement, there are now many pre-packaged solutions currently available in the market, and the number of such solutions continues to expand.

We can start reviewing security with one of the great strengths of the Internet, the fact that most communication is based on open standards. When it comes to security, this is its greatest flaw.

Security has several different aspects: access, data, protocols, information and transactions. Most security systems address two or more of these categories. All security systems involve some method of keeping information hidden from third parties who should not have access. Today we take a lot of security for granted, credit card transactions in the store, at the gas station, electronic banking at the ATM, direct debits and deposits at our banks. Yet, many individuals remain concerned about security breaches and scams on, or via, the Internet.

Encryption, authentication and message integrity explained

Three fundamental aspects of security systems you need to understand are *encryption, authentication* and *message integrity*. Each of these serves an important role in the development of secure systems.

The encryption process encodes the data in a way that only the sender and the target recipient can understand. Most encryption schemes use two components, an algorithm and either one or two keys. An algorithm is a mathematical process that uses the key to scramble the data in a unique way. In a single key system, the same key is used both to encode and to decode the data. The keys to "unlock" the data are provided to recipients according to specific application needs. Dual key systems use both a public and a private key. This pair of keys is generated mathematically in such a way that a message encoded with one can *only* be decoded with the other. The public key is usually deposited electronically in a secure facility, e.g., a bank or other trusted institution, and is available to anyone who wants it. You retain the private key to encrypt and decrypt messages. The mathematics used in the public key/private key scenario have the added benefit of validating that you are the person originating the transaction or the message. (It is very easy for a hacker to "fake" your identity in some applications like email, thereby creating the illusion that email was sent by someone who in fact did not send it at all.)

Authentication is a method to identify that the sender and receiver of a transaction on the Internet are who they claim to be. We verify the authentic nature of the participants so that a transfer or transaction may take place.

> Smart answers to tough questions
>
> Q: What is encryption?
> A: Encryption is the process of converting data into a form that is unreadable by unauthorized users.

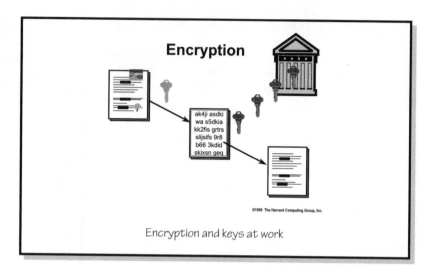

Encryption

ak4ji asdki
wa s5dkia
kk2fis grtrs
slijsifs 9r8
b66 3kdid
skixsn geq

©1999 The Harvard Computing Group, Inc.

Encryption and keys at work

Message integrity involves adding a checksum to each message to ensure that the contents are not altered in transit. The sending software calculates the checksum and appends it to the transmitted message. The receiving software computes the check sum and compares the results of its calculation with the checksum in the message. If they are equal, there is a high probability that the message received is the same as the message sent.

> **Smart things to say about e-commerce**
>
> Authentication is a method to identify that the sender and receiver of a transaction on the Internet are authorized to complete the transaction.

The basic principles of encryption, authentication and integrity provide the foundation of most Internet security systems, although they are available in a variety of forms according to the complexity and transaction needs of the e-commerce systems. Most security systems use one or more of the standards listed in the table below.

SOME IMPORTANT INTERNET SECURITY STANDARDS FOR E-COMMERCE		
Standard	Function	e-commerce use
SSL (Secure Sockets Layer)	Provides security for the data packets at the network layer	Applications using browsers, web servers and Internet systems
S-HTTP (Secure HTTP)	Security at the web transaction level	Applications using browsers, web servers and Internet systems
PGP	Provides encryption and weak authentication for e-mail transmitted across the Internet	Secure email transmission for important information
Secure MIME (S/MIME)	Security for e-mail attachments across various platforms	Secure email applications with encryption and digital signature
Secure Electronic Transaction (SET)	Security for credit card transactions	e-commerce payments and debits

A good way to picture e-commerce security is to view the network of computers and customers that you want to communicate with as the first stage, then layer the business functions that are needed to make the system operational. This may not make you a security expert, but you'll be smart enough to develop a security strategy based on the way that you want your business to operate.

Smart quotes

You can go and find a mailbox right now, open the door to a tin box, tin door, no lock, with unencrypted information in English, sealed in a paper-thin envelope with spit, yet people are worried about online privacy.

Scott McNealy (Chairman, Sun Microsystems)

Many organizations are unwilling to implement secure electronic mail systems as it makes day-to-day work practices more difficult. This is despite the fact that much of the content is confidential in nature. A single mistake in the email system could (probably will) send the data to the wrong individual. Many law suits and other personnel problems have resulted from these simple security mishaps.

Firewalls

A Firewall is used as a way of preventing unwanted users and data from getting into the corporate network or Intranet. A firewall implements access controls based on the contents of the packets of data that are trans-

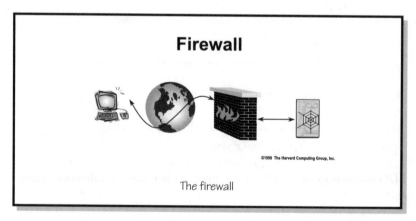

Firewall

©1999 The Harvard Computing Group, Inc.

The firewall

Q: Will a firewall protect me from virus attacks?
A: No, firewalls are designed to keep unauthorized visitors and data from your systems. They do not protect again viruses. Separate software systems are needed to scan for viruses before information is transferred inside the firewall.

Smart answers to tough questions

mitted between the parties and devices on the network. Valid participants are allowed in and the firewall will provide protection against unauthorized outsiders. Smart people think of a firewall as a software barrier between their network and the outside world.

The word "firewall" is now often used to describe a variety of security issues, but strictly speaking, it only performs part of these functions. Use it in conjunction with other security measures such as authentication and digital signatures and you'll have a comprehensive range of access control and security systems.

By combining these elements and a secure networking protocol, companies and their partners can create virtual private networks. These networks can be used as if there were physical networks, but the interconnectivity is leased from other suppliers or occurs across the Internet.

Transactions

Another important area for Internet security is the transaction. Most of the transaction systems on the marketplace are based on technology known as Electronic Data Interchange (EDI).

EDI systems provide the vehicle for input, authentication, validation, agreement and electronic payments to occur in a matter of seconds over a net-

Smart things
to say about
e-commerce

EDI: electronic data interchange

The controlled transfer of data between businesses and organizations via established security standards.

work. In the past, EDI systems were very expensive to implement, in part because each EDI initiative typically required a custom-built network or leased time and bandwidth on a public EDI network. The high costs of EDI limited its use to larger companies who could justify the significant cost associated with the development of the system. More recently, EDI systems are being implemented over the Internet. As with many things Internet blessed, the cost and accessibility of this technology is affordable to everyone, including the smallest business operating from home. Describing EDI in detail is beyond the scope of this book for those interested in more information on this complex topic, go to our suggested reading on the subject in the glossary.

Many transactions are handled via the SSL and S-HTTP protocols. Having created a secure mechanism to conduct business with a close to standard browser, many merchants and vendors use them extensively.

SET: *secure electronic transaction*

The Secure Electronic Transaction (SET) is another standard in the EDI space, This standard is designed to allow merchant transactions to occur across the Internet. As with a traditional transaction, the customer needs to have a valid account set up, then they receive a valid certificate with a public key to authenticate the transaction. Before merchants can process a transaction, they need to have certificates that contain both the banks and their own public keys. Now we are ready to start the transaction process.

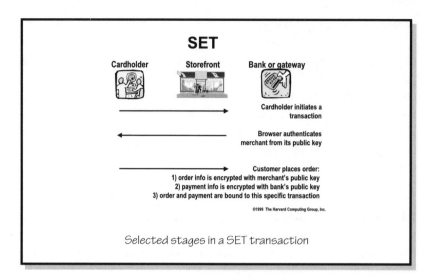

SET

Cardholder   Storefront   Bank or gateway

Cardholder initiates a
transaction

Browser authenticates
merchant from its public key

Customer places order:
1) order info is encrypted with merchant's public key
2) payment info is encrypted with bank's public key
3) order and payment are bound to this specific transaction

©1999 The Harvard Computing Group, Inc.

Selected stages in a SET transaction

The cardholder starts the transaction within the store on the Internet and the browser authenticates the merchant from its public key (and vice versa). Then the customer is ready to place the order and the order is encrypted. Payment information is also encrypted, but with the bank's public key, and both sessions are bound together in the transaction.

Once the price and the product information are in process, the merchant verifies the customer's digital signature and then sends the order to the bank with their own certificate and payment information. At the end of the process the bank verifies the merchant's signature and payment component of the message and then authorizes payment so the merchant can fill the order.

If this seems familiar to many other "store" transactions, this should not be a surprise. It is designed to be very similar to normal "store" transactions.

Other technology groups

Most of the technology needed to develop e-commerce can be grouped into four categories, application development tools being the foundation of any web-based system. Most systems provide the technical platforms for system development and deployment. However, specialized systems have emerged into the marketplace over the last two years, dramatically reducing the time and effort needed to develop sophisticated e-commerce systems.

Authoring tools and content management

Today there are a number of authoring tools to choose from, ranging from the very popular visual products from Microsoft and other leading firms, right through to database-driven systems.

Most e-commerce systems today need to customize data and the interaction with the system. The components you must have are:

- a web server

- application development tools

- a database to drive the system

- authoring and maintenance tools.

As the web server is the publishing center of any e-commerce system, it becomes the final delivery vehicle for information input to the system. An effective way of dealing with these large volumes of data is to store the information in databases that can be accessed through the web browser.

EXAMPLES OF TECHNOLOGY COMPONENTS FOR E-COMMERCE SYSTEM SELECTION

Application development	Content management	Security and transactions	Hosting and server management
Authoring tools	Managing and updating of information	Digital signatures	Bandwidth
Web servers	Version/revision control	SET	Security
Web development platforms	Personalization	Email	24 × 7 operation
Browser	Self service applications	Inventory linking (ERP systems)	Internal/external
Network tools	International language support	Firewalls	Administration and optimization tools
Databases	Corporate Portal systems	Remote access	Remote administration
Integration tools	Information feeds and services	EDI	Monitoring and performance tools

Source: Harvard Computing Group.

In many cases companies need a good way of being able to deal easily with the management, updating and modifying content inside these databases. Because of this demand, Content Management Systems have emerged on the market. These systems allow for the easy modification, updating and distribution of information and tasks between different components of the e-commerce solution.

Content management system purchases are driven by the need for electronic business or e-commerce. The types of applications being developed include catalogs and product information sites, business to business applications, self-service and customer service applications. These usually require careful control and presentation of information to provide the most value to the target consumer. At the same time, they also require close control of the update, release, and approval processes for the information on the site. These systems provide information flow through the e-commerce solution.

Customers using content management systems need control and speed. They also want quality and customization of both content and appearance. Fortunately, with the modular nature of many Content Management Systems, it is possible to have it all.

Content Management Systems provide the business controls to:

- manage the data presentation

- enable distributed updating

- make posting new changes fast yet customized.

Options

One decision that many firms are faced with today is whether to go with a document, publishing or business oriented system. While for some applications the choice may not make a difference, others will clearly benefit from a particular selection. The examples in the table below should help you decide.

EXAMPLES OF CONTENT MANAGEMENT ALTERNATIVES AND WHERE TO USE THEM

Customer application	Application characteristics	Best suited system
Technical publishing, database publishing, knowledge management applications	High volume electronic document applications. Built in sophisticated information retrieval and PDF generation	Document oriented content management
Catalogs, business to business applications, supply chain and distribution applications	Customization of content and presentation can be controlled interactively. Business rules can be developed and modified easily. High level of personalization	Business oriented content management
Commercial publishing, electronic magazines and personalized content	Customized content can be presented in many different forms and formats	Publishing oriented content management

Knowledge management

Ask your colleagues what "e-commerce" means and you will get many answers. Knowledge Management is the same. One way of looking at e-commerce systems is that they are computers that make or save money. By this definition Knowledge Management systems become the food that supplies these systems.

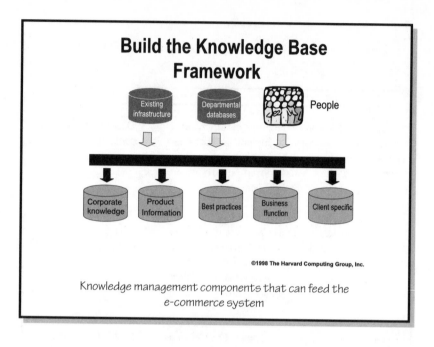

Build the Knowledge Base Framework

Existing infrastructure

Departmental databases

People

Corporate knowledge

Product Information

Best practices

Business ffunction

Client specific

©1998 The Harvard Computing Group, Inc.

Knowledge management components that can feed the e-commerce system

Knowledge management systems and tools are used to capture, re-use and re-purpose the relevant information to the person that needs it, preferably at the time they need it. They can be as simple as a frequently asked questions (FAQ) application, providing the right information to a client in need of on-line customer support. It could also be as complex as linking into a knowledge management repository of relevant information for a service engineer on the line. Many help desk systems and support costs associated with them would be impossible to implement without this technology. Many KM systems are also based on groupware applications to share information between departments and individuals in the enterprise. These are usually easily integrated into e-commerce strategies and systems.

Taxation

E-commerce systems will often use specialized software designed to calculate and segment the taxable elements of the transaction. Many vendors of e-commerce systems have their own taxation package, or they relicense and integrate software from vendors who specialize in this subject. Today, it is relatively easy to acquire and integrate taxation software. Nevertheless, take care if you are in the international marketplace that the systems chosen meet all of the collection rules and options that are permissible and required.

XML (*extensible markup language*)

XML is such an important standard in the development of e-commerce systems that smart people need to know about it. XML was officially born in December 1997 and is the result of a working group funded by the world wide web consortium (W3C) and various vendors. In some ways, XML was born out of frustration, with developers and users of complex web applications stymied by the limits of HTML. XML is now a standard that addresses many of these concerns. It may become the standard that finally links web and database publishing activities in a common framework. XML has all the benefits of HTML and more. The table below illustrates the power that XML brings and, if there are features that you would like to add, it's as simple as extending the language.

Databases, publishing and presentation

These three primary elements influence almost all web-based applications today. Many organizations are wrestling with the major issue of formulating a cohesive strategy for information maintenance and publishing. Those organizations on the cutting edge are having the greatest problems.

HTML	XML
• HTML describes the content of the document and has no application control over presentation • Usually only easily readable with a browser • Non-extensible mark up • No context or access control	• XML describes the format, presentation and provides application control over the content of the document • Documents can be read, exchanged and manipulated with many applications • Extensible markup language to create industry and client specific applications • Context and access control

Source: ©1999 Harvard Computing Group.

Many of the current systems developed to date, have used ODBC and custom programming to produce sophisticated solutions. However, it is not a pretty sight under the covers. Most systems are hard wired to these databases, and the much-desired flexibility of platform independence is absent. XML and the associated XSL (stylesheets) could change it all.

XML provides a bridge between the publishing, database and web presentation world in a way that has not occurred before. Bridge technologies take off when market conditions demand, often as a de facto standard.

XML allows new things to develop that were just not previously feasible. Despite the fact that SGML defined a separate style and content model, individual control over elements was not available to most databases to filter, manipulate or combine them. XML will make this accessible to many systems, providing parameter-based searching and reordering in the pre-

XML	Existing industry standards
• Permits export of information to hard copy printable media	• Portable Document Format (PDF)
• Allows control of content based on application needs	• None
• Allows text search to be based on the context of information sought	• None
• Data oriented style and content independence	• SGML
• Centralized link management for URL updates	• None

Source: ©1999 Harvard Computing Group

sentation of results. The precision of the major search applications will be dramatically improved compared to today's implementations.

XML is significant because of the technical barriers it overcomes and powerful business requirements it supports. The reasons below illustrate some of the adoption benefits that you can expect because of XML development currently occurring in the industry.

These are the business reasons to consider XML based technology

- We can re-use and re-purpose information quickly and efficiently.
- We can reduce the maintenance costs associated with our e-commerce solution.
- We can design flexibility into the system, making it easier when we want to make change as our business requirements dictate.
- We will be able to share information easily inside our organization and with our business partners.

Smart things to say about e-commerce

XML is gaining support as an industry standard for information exchange between various systems in the marketplace.

Now that we have dealt with the major issues of where data is and how it is managed, there are a few other areas that you may want to consider to make your e-commerce system really fly.

Pulling technology components together

Bringing your technology components together in a common framework is not as difficult as you may think. The challenge is to ensure that you have an up to date view of the market. Each niche in the marketplace has software and hardware companies creating packaged solutions to get you to market faster. Unfortunately, there is no better way of staying current than continuous monitoring of the marketplace. If you don't, you may spend more than you need on a particular solution, or even worse be less competitive because of maintenance overheads that have been cut by innovative new technologies.

OK, you have had your fill of technology for now, let's start exploring how we can apply what we are learning. Our starting place will be one class of customers, the electronic consumer.

4

Electronic Consumers – Attracting, Predicting and Engaging Them

The electronic consumer is a special type of customer for web-based marketing. Unlike business to business users, where we can often identify a group of users with specific characteristics, electronic consumers are different. This creates some technical and marketing challenges.

To begin with, some fundamentals of web based marketing will help you position your activities to best meet their needs. As the demographics of the web become broader, different classes of consumer have started to operate in various parts of it. In the early days many started out as consumers of information, which is one reason why the search sites became the primary landmark for many of them.

During the web's early years, from 1995 to 1998, users started at a search web site to identify interesting places to go, specifically to find relevant information. (This continues to remain a problem.) A cadre of web sites including, Yahoo, Lycos, Excite, HotBot, AltaVista, and OpenText were the main draws at this time.

Although these sites continue to grow in popularity in terms of volume, the balance of power has shifted. The top 10 search sites, drawing almost 80% of the traffic two years ago, today are responsible for barely more than 50% of total traffic. An important change illustrating a more sophisticated use of the web.

Who are the consumers, and where are they?

It is important for us to understand the demographics of the web, particularly when you determine a strategy that will attract consumers. We should look at how current consumers are operating, but we must also see where the trends are leading us.

As a caveat to demographics, we have used various sources and statistics in this book. There is a wide discrepancy in numbers and estimates from the various research and consulting sources. Interestingly enough, most of the very large numbers that were predicted by researchers a couple of years ago, have turned out to be relatively conservative in terms of market growth (something that does not normally happen with market estimates). This just goes to show how quickly things change in this market. New products and the way that they are delivered can and have made new markets.

With a vast international community of users and potential consumers, the Internet offers an opportunity that merchants and suppliers of information and services have never seen before. Today the majority of users are still located in North America and Europe. However, new markets are

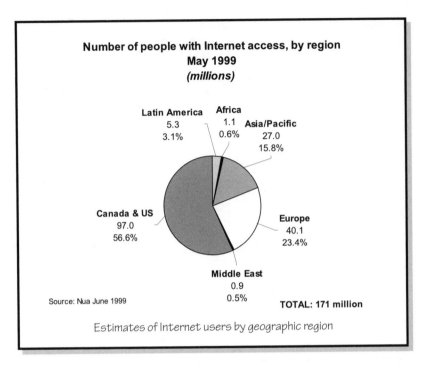

Number of people with Internet access, by region
May 1999
(millions)

Latin America — 5.3 — 3.1%

Africa — 1.1 — 0.6%

Asia/Pacific — 27.0 — 15.8%

Canada & US — 97.0 — 56.6%

Europe — 40.1 — 23.4%

Middle East — 0.9 — 0.5%

Source: Nua June 1999

TOTAL: 171 million

Estimates of Internet users by geographic region

also coming on strong as the impact of the Internet continues to grow. The numbers of users continue to expand across the globe.

For the development of the marketplace, obviously the growth and so-phistication of patterns of users will determine how quickly expansion and adoption will happen. The snapshot above, taken as part of a US Government e-commerce report in June 1999, illustrates the high percent-age of populations now gaining on-line access. This will ultimately pro-vide the foundation for the growth of the industry.

The most popular activities of users continue to be email, finding informa-tion about a hobby, and general news. These continue to outrank on-line

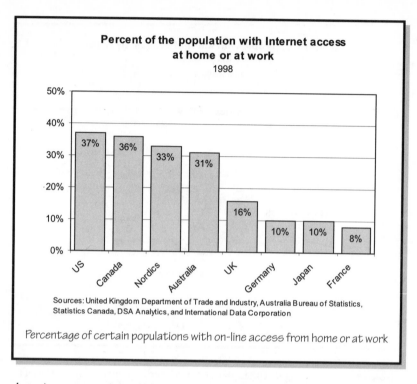

Percent of the population with Internet access at home or at work
1998

Sources: United Kingdom Department of Trade and Industry, Australia Bureau of Statistics, Statistics Canada, DSA Analytics, and International Data Corporation

Percentage of certain populations with on-line access from home or at work

shopping as an activity. However, on-line shopping is growing in popularity. As it becomes easier to facilitate the delivery of goods and services using the Internet and associated overnight shipment services, the convenience of shopping on the Internet is catching on fast.

Services that would not have been considered reasonable to purchase a few years ago are becoming popular. However most of the sales to date are in books, CDs, software, high tech and other easy to shop for and deliver to the consumer. The range of offerings is likely to expand dramatically as groceries, financial services and even on-line house hunting expand their current small penetration of the marketplace.

Early adopters

Group of consumers that start using technology and systems early in their introduction to the marketplace.

Smart things
to say about
e-commerce

With more than 92 million users of the Internet in North America alone, and an estimated 171 worldwide, the marketplace has exploded to provide a very high level of actual and potential business for merchants. At the same time, the expansion in offerings of different types of products and services has made it very attractive for many consumers to become enamored with the opportunity and convenience of shopping on-line.

Users are becoming more sophisticated and are moving on from the first typical applications that attracted them to the Internet, typically email and web browsing for research.

The trends also indicate that more and more users are not just browsing or using email, but are in fact shopping on the Internet. Of those 55 million that are shopping, more than half (28 million) are buying as well.

Smart things
to say about e-commerce

With a market of approaching 200 million worldwide, as Internet users turn become Internet shoppers and consumers, huge changes in purchasing patterns will occur.

Recent polls taken show the typical applications and activities of digital consumers, and have shown the buying patterns shown in the table below.

Many consumers continue to visit on-line stores to ensure that they effectively research their purchases before they buy. As more organizations offer exacting information about products and services, the web is becoming the location of choice to obtain purchase information.

SMART VOICES

DIGITAL CONSUMERS

Buying habits of 2400 "digital consumers" over recent 90 day period:

- 41% participated in an online auction;
- 26% bought computer software;
- 25% banked online;
- 25% bought books;
- 23% bought airline tickets;
- 12% made hotel or travel arrangements; and
- 12% traded stocks, bonds or mutual funds.

Keeping an eye on consumer groups and trends

Many firms have spent a lot of money watching what has been happening in the marketplace and are adjusting their strategies accordingly. On the Internet, you need to be a little more aggressive and predictive. You don't want to miss out totally on a new trend or class of buyer in the market-place.

The fact that many of the research firms have been incorrect in their assumptions about the e-commerce marketplace underlines the need to watch the market. Understand the demographics and buying patterns in your market and use them to revise your e-strategy.

Smart things
to say about
e-commerce

About consumers:

While many consumers are still making their purchases in a "brick and mortar store" much of the research and decision making process is being done on-line in advance of the purchase.

1998	2002
8.4 million users	16.6 million users
$16.6 million spending	$1.2 billion spending
Source: Jupiter Communications.	

A good example of this type of work was some recent research on on-line teenagers published in the Industry Standard. This study showed the trends listed in the table above.

In addition to this dramatic increase in the number of teenagers on-line, the predicted growth of almost 2000% in their on-line spending habits should get your attention. These population groups will continue to modify their on-line behavior over the coming years. Make sure that you are ready to reach them.

Observing industry trends on the Internet is an effective way of ensuring that you do not miss out on big opportunities. As we'll see later, it's risky to do nothing but watch the market develop and then come in when some buying patterns and demand are in place.

To stay current on industry trends:

- subscribe to leading industry magazines
- visit the Internet research sites regularly
- subscribe to industry specific newsletter and newsgroups.

Smart things to say about e-commerce

Retaining and engaging consumers

Building a client base that will meet your needs on the web is obviously "first base" for any strategy involving digital consumers.

Once you have established the prospects for your product, test the market, particularly if you plan to make this a mainstream initiative for your company.

In general, companies look at the web in two ways. First, to find better ways of dealing with their current clientele, and second, to expand their customer base significantly. Many of the tactics and techniques we will review can be applied toward both goals. However, the amount of energy expended, and the potential costs associated with the latter option could be very significant. Much of what we have learned about web customers confirms our experience with traditional means of acquiring and managing relationships. It costs lots of money to acquire each customer, and once you have them and can keep them satisfied, they are likely to come back. No rocket science here. However, when you apply many of the bulk marketing techniques common to US and European marketing strategies, some bad things happen. By working the percentages, we assume that we will have results based on volume and filtering of potential prospects. Consequently, we tend to use familiar media mechanisms such as direct mail and telemarketing, targeting a group that will meet certain demographic criteria such as:

- age group

- hobbies and special interests

- professional affiliations

- marital status

- industry

- educational affiliations

- title and decision making profile

- earning power

- a user of product that would make them a prospect.

These profiles would then be further processed, until we end up with a number of "qualified leads" to go to the next stage. These leads are often handled by internal sales teams on the telephone, and then forwarded to field account reps for appointments (or they could be handled directly on the telephone depending on the product or service).

Consequently, we lean toward this approach of targeting, contacting, filtering, distributing and then following up accordingly. If we lived in an ideal world:

- we would not send unsolicited mail that would either not reach, or annoy the recipient;

- more of the "follow up" calls would occur at the right time in the sales cycle;

- we would not "lose leads" because we did not have the staff to follow up on them;

- field sales staff would not "cherry pick" the leads they wanted; and

Smart things
to say about
e-commerce

> Push
>
> Delivery of information to potential consumers.

- we would not target the wrong user, or provide them with the inappropriate product causing the process to fail.

Unfortunately, we all know that these things do happen on a regular basis, and when they do, the sales process ends in failure.

Most of the techniques we have described could be considered a "push" marketing effort. Although we tend to consider push as a web phenomenon, we have in fact been pushing stuff to prospects and clients for many years.

Now that we understand some of the problems with our traditional marketing approach, we can review what excites consumers on the Internet and where the potential pitfalls are in courting them electronically.

In cyberspace, clients can close the door and slam the phone down very fast. Internet consumers are not patient (unless you are the only game in town). Understanding what makes them excited and what turns them off

Smart things
to say about
e-commerce

> About Internet consumers:
>
> - They can slam the door on you without you knowing.
> - They can leave the room quickly.
> - They can leave the room quietly.
> - They are likely to tell others about their experience.
> - They will tell more people if the experience is negative.

> Content is what will determine long-term Internet profitability. To focus on technology without content is like building a hospital without nurses and doctors.
>
> Ed Horowitz (Leader, e-Citi division, Citigroup)

Smart quotes

so quickly is obviously critical to success. One thing we know for sure is that Internet consumers love good content. If I provide good content, then they are likely to stay at my site and see more of what I have to offer. If the content is bad, unless there is some other tremendous reason to be on my site, they will not only leave, but are very unlikely to return. Most of our companies and organizations spend a significant amount of time and money trying to find ways to get people to our sites in the first place. However, if consumers "bail out" quickly after viewing our sites, then all that marketing effort has been for naught.

Content is king. Study after study continues to emphasize this as the number one factor for return visits to web sites.

Understanding who is visiting your site and why is vital to your strategy. There are different types of visitors – customers, prospects, partners and

About content:

- Good content is the #1 reason people return to web sites.
- 75% of 8,600 respondents cited content as the reason for return visits.
- Other reasons for return visits included ease of use, quick download time, and frequent updates.

Source: Forrester Research

Smart things to say about e-commerce

the press. It is important that each of these has a fulfilling experience. Determining which ones are most important and how best to make this experience have useful outcomes for your business will start you on the right road for development of your web environment.

Remembering your business goals and linking them to the experience of visiting the site will help.

Attracting potential customers is one thing. Retaining them is another. You must encourage consumer loyalty. This is not something that can be done as a part of a simple web marketing effort. Rather it has to be built into the fabric of sales and marketing efforts. Building this type of loyalty can be very effective for the development of a long-term effective strategy on the web.

> **Smart things to say about e-commerce**
>
> Create value by offering redeemable coupons or rebates to consumers, and make them available only on your web site.

This type of program will replace the "event" marketing so common to early web efforts. Many firms will promise a high level of traffic in a short period, but what use will this be if your consumers "bail out" after a short time on the site?

Here are some good ideas to assist with the development of loyalty from your e-commerce site.

Create value

When someone visits your site give him or her something of value. Creating value is one of the most important aspects to create loyalty. It provides a reason for returning and can be very simple. Offer redeemable coupons or rebates to consumers, and make them available only on your web site. Airlines have been using this to great effect in their craving to get consumers to sign up and purchase tickets on-line. Moreover, it is working. In the

US, many fares are only available via the web, and sometimes at a much lower cost than the traditional travel agent can offer.

Convenience

Make your site easier than doing business anywhere else. Even purchasing an automobile can now be made easier on the web. Information sites such as carpoint.com have almost as much (in some cases more) information about cars than you can find on the automakers' own web sites. TicketMaster, a supplier of concert and event tickets, has increased its web presence and revenue considerably over the past year. This is most certainly due to the tremendous convenience of this service. In addition to the ease of signing up and getting information on the web, there are usually no telephone lines or operators to wait for, all of which contribute to an experience of convenience.

Confidence

Building confidence for your visitors is a good method to improve traffic and loyalty. If a brand is already established, such as the Wall Street Journal, there is not much work required to make that translate to the web environment. But new brands and sites need to build the confidence of their users before they will return time and again.

Entertainment value

Creating entertainment also offers a good way of bringing consumers back. Sometimes this can be as simple as a joke of the day.

Reward

Giving something away is used extensively as a way of creating and sustaining traffic. It does not have to be expensive. JellyBelly.com gives away free jelly beans to users who complete an on-line survey at their web site. The survey is offered at different times every day. Consumers have to keep coming back to try to get to the survey and win the free samples.

Customer Service

Outstanding customer service for your consumer is one of the most important aspects of any e-commerce experience. Last year, our consulting firm purchased an enterprise network computer via an on-line auction at www.onsale.com (now merged with egghead.com). The server arrived within the 5 days advertised, but unfortunately without a critical circuit board that was part of the original order. The total order was for around $2,500 but the component that was missing had a cost of around $2,000. (It was a good deal!) Onsale.com also found that they were out of stock of the missing item. The resolution? Onsale.com had us purchase the item directly from the manufacturer and reimbursed us with a credit to our account. This type of service, even when you obviously lose money on the sale, creates confidence and loyalty that runs beyond any single deal.

Smart quotes

Electronic selling and purchasing are going to be the default method of doing business, not the special case.

Stu Feldman (Director, IBM Institute for Advanced Commerce)

Smart things to say about e-commerce

Develop loyalty on your web site through:

- value
- convenience
- confidence
- entertainment value
- rewards
- customer service.

Targeted marketing strategies

Development of your own targeted marketing strategy to address consumer needs is a great way to gain the results you want and avoid the problems. Because the consumer base is huge on the web, and the cost of reaching it is low, you need to employ targeted marketing strategies and techniques.

Targeted marketing programs align the needs of specific sectors of the market with exact matches for the product or service that you plan to present. In recent years, these sorts of programs have become very popular. One of the major reasons is the lower cost of obtaining and retaining clients.

Electronic mail is the least expensive method of targeting information to meet a specific prospect's profile. Compare these contact costs:

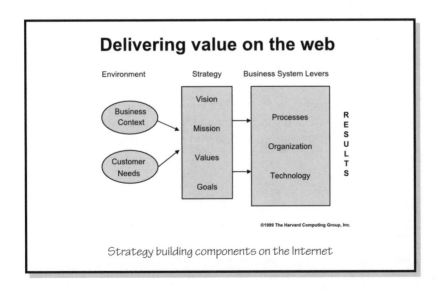

Delivering value on the web

Environment   Strategy   Business System Levers

Business Context

Customer Needs

Vision

Mission

Values

Goals

Processes

Organization

Technology

RESULTS

©1999 The Harvard Computing Group, Inc.

Strategy building components on the Internet

Targeted marketing

Development of marketing programs by identifying segments in specific markets and designing the product or service to specifically meet these needs.

- electronic mail $0.05 per unit

- direct mail $2–$5 per unit

- telephone interview and contact $8–$24 per person

- face-to-face interview $40–$400 per person.

Of all of these, the face-to-face interview is the most expensive. Therefore the better the qualification earlier in the process, the better the chance we have of producing sales that are more suited to the business situation. Targeted marketing can dramatically cut the cost of sales, while at the same time reducing the time required to complete the sale. The Internet is a very effective way of cutting prospecting time and costs.

Start a targeted marketing program by segmenting and test marketing the potential client base. This will give you information related to the target consumer and how best to reach them via various Internet marketing programs.

Once you have selected the target base, think about ways to reach it.

Direct email

Direct email with a customized message is one of the most effective ways of delivering information to your potential targets. Today there are a myriad of tools and programs out there to help you with the development of your targeted program.

Smart things
to say about e-commerce

Electronic Mail is the least expensive method of targeting information to meet a specific prospect's profile

It is important not to confuse targeted email and "spam". Spammers, next to confidence tricksters and pedophiles, are rated in the top categories of hated activities on the Internet. You do not want to be a member of this group. The "junk mail" that they produce is the scourge of Internet service providers, hosting services and corporate MIS depart- ments around the world. Development of email programs should always meet privacy standards and be respectful of target organizations' email policies. (Many firms have very good screening software that will stop email coming in from a particular domain name if you do not comply.)

Building your own email list, and using an email mail list server can be a great way of ensuring that consumers proactively subscribe to offers and information about your products without a lot of sales effort. A signifi-

---

Direct email programs:

- select a list that has the target names, positions that you need;
- develop the copy carefully;
- allow users to "remove" themselves from any targeted email list;
- allow other users to easily "subscribe" to lists, so that email can be for-warded to interested parties;
- if you are going to make this part of a series to a target base, try and automate the process using specialized email software;
- HTML mail systems can include graphics and a more personalized version of the materials (take care as not all of your prospects may use HTML compatible email software); and
- never use Spam methods.

Smart things
to say about
e-commerce

Smart things
to say about
e-commerce

Spamming

The indiscriminate sending of large amounts of junk email to a very broad audience, knowing that a large amount of the consumers will not want to receive the material.

cant community of interested parties can be built in a relatively short period of time, and users can add or remove themselves without the need for much maintenance in the process. This self-policing method is non-intrusive and avoids putting people off before you start any form of business relationship with them.

Bulletin boards, newsgroups and threaded discussion groups

Another effective method of creating sales and general interest in a product or service is the bulletin board or threaded discussion group. Users can proactively sign up for more information or a specific service.

In today's climate it is reasonable to allow visitors to a site to decide if they want to be added to another list as a result of participating in a discussion group. Naturally you need to maintain the privacy of each member of these groups. Most professional or hobby bulletin boards and related Newsgroups specifically request that members do no soliciting. However, less scrupulous companies and individuals often ignore these requests. A good rule of thumb is to treat each one of these areas just as you would want to be treated yourself.

Roboting and gathering intelligence on web visitors

Robots are yet another means to gain information on consumers. When a visitor to a site clicks on a certain section, system monitoring software will

Roboting	Smart things to say about e-commerce
Equipping web sites with software that captures demographic information about visitors.	

capture the location where the visitor has come from. In many cases much more information than this can be collected, including email addresses.

Most organizations now use technology to help them understand how many visitors they have, where they have come from, how long they stayed and which path they took through the site. You can even collect the visitor's email address, which you could then use to generate automated email "follow up" to the visit. This can be a very powerful tool if used appropriately, but many visitors will view this as an invasion of their privacy, especially if you don't tell them in advance what you are doing. I recommend that you make it clear the privacy standards that your site and organization uses. You may want to consider an "opt-in" policy for mailing lists and other information, rather than adding people to your lists without asking first.

Other traffic building techniques

Increasing the traffic to your web site is key to the success of your e-commerce site. After all, we know that creating web traffic is not purely a "build it and they will come" slam-dunk.

A combination of these programs will build the traffic on your site. The simplest of all is to register with search engines. There is no question that many Internet consumers still rely on a major search engine or portal to help them find the things they are looking for. We have all been spammed

Smart things
to say about
e-commerce

Build web traffic through:

- appropriate registration at the search engines
- content partnerships
- banner advertising
- press relations
- web-based events.

to death by companies and services offering to make us number 1 on the results list for fees ranging from $50 on up. Marketing companies offer these services on a continuous basis. Acquiring a spider to assist with the placement and registration of your site to the larger search engines is also a worthwhile expense. Many of the software products that the professionals use at Internet Service Providers and marketing firms are available to the public for a very modest fee.

Another method is RealNames[tm]. You can purchase keywords on the web via the realnames.com web site. RealNames avoid the need for www prefixes on web sites, and allow users that have their browser connect directly to their target site. In the long term, this could become a very popular method of navigating and attracting consumers to your site. If you purchase the right to a "RealName" you can link it directly to the appropriate part of your web site. For example if you were working for Ford Motor, you could acquire Ford Explorer as a RealName, and then type the

Smart things
to say about
e-commerce

Spider

A tool to automate the indexing and registration of your site with popular search engines to ensure that your content is indexed.

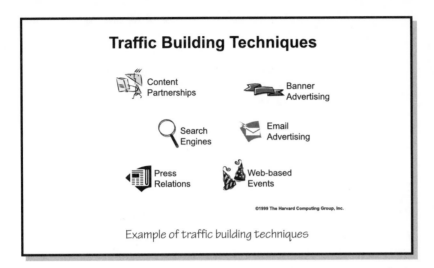

Traffic Building Techniques

Content Partnerships

Banner Advertising

Search Engines

Email Advertising

Press Relations

Web-based Events

©1999 The Harvard Computing Group, Inc.

Example of traffic building techniques

key words *Ford Explorer* on your browser. You would then be directed specifically to the Explorer web page, with no HTML address needed.

A content partnership is another great way to improve the quality of the consumer experience on your site, as good content can keep them coming back. Combine this with a community strategy to create real interest in your site.

Advertising is one more way of driving traffic to your site if you know where your prospects are going. Today most advertising is still operating

Impression

A single view of an element of a web page; often referred to for advertising measurements on the web when each impression represents the presentation and viewing of an on-line advertisement.

Smart things to say about e-commerce

**Smart things
to say about
e-commerce**

Click throughs

Click throughs are when advertisers not only see the ads that have been
served up on the web site, but they actually "click through" to visit the site
or offer linked to the ad. This is the equivalent of "going into the store".

on a CPM basis. Depending on the web site on which you want to adver-
tise, it could cost you anywhere from $25 to $75 per thousand impressions. Unfortunately, this does not guarantee that others will actually click
on your advertisement and thereby come to your site, it just means they
will see the ad. Due to a relatively low click-through rate it is likely that
more and more advertisers will be more discerning and move to either
more specialized sites where higher click-throughs are likely, or start paying for advertising on a different basis.

Some advertising firms are now starting to offer advertising based on the
number of click-throughs to the advertiser site. Although the price will be
considerably higher for this option, it is likely that more advertisers will
start to move in this direction as it provides real visitors, not just "visibility" for the advertiser. Web based events also keep users coming back for
more at your site. Try competitions, delivery of reports, seminars and other
useful programs that will help make the visit worthwhile.

Press relations are another way of making the site an interesting place to
go. Investors, analysts, consultants and clients are often curious to know

**Smart things
to say about
e-commerce**

CPM

Cost per thousand impressions; a measurement of how many times someone has viewed your banner ad via a browser.

Relationship marketing

- allows you on the Internet to present your offerings in a very personalized way that is impossible with traditional means, or traditional costs; and
- offers a unique method of customizing a product offering around a particular consumer's needs.

Smart things
to say about
e-commerce

how things are going. The press releases can also be an unobtrusive way of delivering news without being too obvious.

Relationship marketing

After you've mastered targeted marketing and the technology available in the marketplace you are now ready to start relationship marketing.

Relationship marketing comprises many components including, one-to-one marketing, personalization, communities, customization and customer relationship management. (As an all-embracing term, CRM probably describes the entire process most completely, although here we are dealing only with marketing aspects of this process, and not the total customer management experience.)

Relationship marketing will allow you to perform incredible feats on the Internet. Never before have we had the opportunity to make up totally new ways of accessing consumers and prospects, while at the same time fine tuning the message and product accordingly to their needs

Customization

Customizing content is one very effective way of ensuring that the right information can be presented to the right group at the right time. With earlier versions of software and systems on the market, this was a very difficult process. As all of the systems that provide customized content capabilities are database driven, providing many different versions of the same materials and still maintaining performance that meets the user needs was very difficult. Today, many systems allow this to occur quickly and easily. For applications where the same data is being presented to different audiences (such as information feeds, catalogs and knowledge management applications), customization becomes a way of life.

It also can be very useful dealing with the different locations of consumers, who may be in different geographic locations or even speaking different languages. Many companies operating in multiple locations offer customization options as consumers enter their site. The experience in the site is then customized to their language, product, pricing and support needs in this target marketplace.

Personalization

Personalization takes customization to the next stage. It builds marketing messaging and web pages based on individuals' specific, personal needs. Software to offer this capability has reached new heights that can include presenting web pages that contain specific product information based on each person's buying patterns, previous visits through the site and how long they stayed in a particular area.

Many individuals perceive that they are being watched while they are out there on the web. They are right, and companies are paying more and more attention to consumer patterns.

Personalization tools allow web merchants and content providers to deliver individual versions of *PC Week* to your desktop, customized auction items and complete sets of products that are specifically focused on your needs. The issues associated with this technology will undoubtedly continue to be a concern for governments, companies and consumer privacy rights groups for the coming years.

Community building

Creating communities on the web has become a popular pastime for merchants in the last 12 months, and for a very good reason. Communities are a great way of providing interesting content that is relevant to your potential client base, and then offering your products as part of the experience.

Earlier in this chapter we reviewed that *content* was king. Many organizations have recognized the value of a community for their clients and prospects and are making money as a result.

A good community site will allow customers to visit repeatedly, without feeling threatened, and to receive useful information relevant to their task and focus. Communities can be built around hobbies, professional interests, vertical applications or other areas of interest.

Developing an effective community site can reduce your customer acquisition costs over the long haul. However, the cost of developing the community site can be considerable in the initial stages, particularly as you will likely have to purchase some content outside the company to keep it

Smart answers to tough questions

Q: Why will a community help my web strategy?
A: Communities are a great way of providing the interesting and useful content to my potential buyers, partners and influencers in our sales strategy.

> *Smart things to say about e-commerce*

Include the following in your community building program:

- email newsletters
- reports relevant to the industry
- community calendars
- public bookmark files
- chat events
- promotions and contests
- community forums and bulletin board
- community knowledge bases.

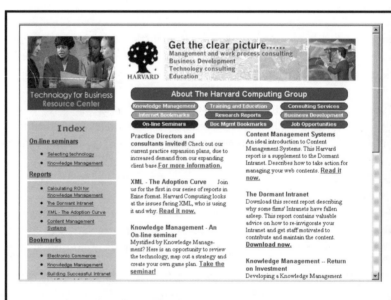

An example of a community focused site, courtesy
Harvard Computing Group, Inc.

interesting. In addition to your benefit of lower customer acquisition costs, your credibility will also increase (providing useful information to your clients will help to establish credibility).

One-to-one marketing

One-to-one marketing has become very popular on the Internet. You should not be surprised, as the earlier elements in this chapter are used extensively in development of a one-to-one marketing strategy. One-to-one allows you to focus your efforts and really target your client base with products that are the best match for each consumer, and with an offer they should not be able to refuse. It also personifies the very best customer retention and management practices created during a long relationship with them, allowing you to receive input and opinions over time and reuse them to the best effect of your company.

Whatever strategies you decide to use for your client base, there is no shortage of tools, assistance and companies that can help in the process. The practices and programs outlined here should help you get pointed in the right direction.

So, determining how and when you are going to attract electronic consumers to your site, keep them coming back, and make the relationship work for the long term, turns out to be more complex than just putting up a web page and licensing the software for the store.

Smart answers to tough questions

> Q: What is one-to-one marketing?
> A: Customization and personalization of your product and prospect's requirements to meet an individual set of established needs. Once matched, a one-to-one marketing program delivers an exact marketing message, with the appropriate product to meet the prospect's needs.

Researching and clearly understanding your target audience, and deciding how you are going to reach them in a consistent and profitable manner needs careful thought. The good news is there are lots of consumers out there, and more are buying directly from the web. As the confidence of Internet consumers increases, and broader services are offered, the opportunity is clear. There are customers out there. All you have to do is find them, interest them, convince them, sell them and, in the process, retrain them.

5

Business to Business E-commerce

(IT IS NOT JUST ABOUT CONSUMERS)

Most e-commerce noise in the news is about the business-to-consumer market. As we reviewed in Chapter 2 this is small potatoes compared to what is happening in the business-to-business e-commerce market. This market is a giant, and one with a very big appetite for growth. Forrester Research now predicts that the business-to-business marketplace will exceed more than $1 trillion by 2003. Comparing this with estimates in the business-to-consumer market over the same period, we could expect more than a 10:1 ratio of revenues.

Smart quotes

Processes are what online business-to-business integration needs to succeed.

Clinton Wilder,
Information Week

Business to business (B2B)

Business to business is all about transactions between your organization

Internet business to business (B2B)

The portion of the market that effects transactions between business operations and their partners in marketing, sales, development, manufacturing and support; this is the largest part of the Internet marketplace, and the fastest growing.

and your partners. Any transactions or information associated with development, manufacturing, delivery, sales and support of products or services is a candidate for a business-to-business system. This broad definition includes many systems that can improve the communications between companies and organizations.

Industries have been using business to business strategies and processes to support the development of their products, services and partnerships for many years. For example, the aerospace industry has been working with partners in the airframe, avionics and engine categories. All of these are members of supply chain groups who co-ordinate design, development, testing, acceptance, production and maintenance of products and systems.

Other industries are moving rapidly into the adoption of supply chain business-to-business systems. In the fall of 1999, the automotive industry announced some major initiatives, including the joint announcement of a huge e-business supply chain program with Ford and Oracle. This will facilitate more than $80 billion dollars in annual purchases and 30,000 suppliers in a single system.

Smart
answers to
tough
questions

Q: What is EDI?
A: Electronic data interchange: the controlled transfer of data between businesses and organizations via established security standards.

EFT

Electronic funds transfer, the secure transfer of funds via an agreed protocol and system.

Smart things
to say about
e-commerce

Today's banking and finance operations have long been dependent on EDI and EFT to ensure that monies and securities are transferred to the company or individual that requested the action. Engineering firms manufacturing products have used business-to-business project management, manufacturing and outsourcing for the development and delivery of their products.

It is likely that you are already using some form of business-to-business system in your organization. Many systems including office suppliers, on-line travel agents and information services, are already online inside many businesses. Some of these have been spectacularly successful.

Supply chain management systems make it possible for participants in the supply chain to see where the production, supply and inventory are in the process. For years, high-tech organizations have been using these business-to-business systems as a way of connecting teams spread about the globe. This has led to the development of *electronic immigration* with

SMART PEOPLE
TO HAVE ON
YOUR SIDE:

TRAVELOCITY.COM

This smart company is a provider and leader in the on-line travel business. Their rapidly growing business to business strategy has won them several awards for service and results. By developing a site that has registered more than of 6.5 million users, the company created loyalty and meteoric sales growth. Their business clients have on-line access to most airlines 42,000 hotels and over 50 car rental firms.

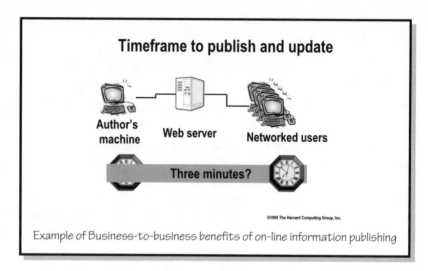

Timeframe to publish and update

Author's machine | Web server | Networked users

Three minutes?

©1999 The Harvard Computing Group, Inc.

Example of Business-to-business benefits of on-line information publishing

outsourced teams of professionals all using a common system. Before the Internet, making connections between these locations required private networks for the groups of collaborators in these business-to-business chains. Despite this cost, the benefit was large enough to warrant large investments in network infrastructure, so companies and organizations set up these private networks to support their business-to-business activities.

However, without the Internet, or some common communications vehicle, the cost of setting these up was high, therefore only the most critical systems were implemented.

Enter the Internet, and things started to change. Companies and organizations set up their own domain names, email servers and supporting systems. As they did so, the communication traffic and patterns between businesses began to change. Your organization is probably already benefiting from these electronic tools. It has now become a natural extension to use

A supplier of information services on the Internet, Intraware.com has grown dramatically providing on-demand information services for their business clients. Having now created a community of interested parties, Intraware has now started to sell products directly on their web site.

SMART PEOPLE TO HAVE ON YOUR SIDE:

INTRAWARE.COM

the same tools for email and transmission of documents between our existing and potential partners and clients.

As the market evolved, it became obvious that other functions used mainly by the "techies" in the organizations, such as FTP and chat were also extremely useful and relevant to business to business users.

The logical step was to extend these systems to our business partners, and yet exclude the public. This caused a new network to emerge. A secure business-to-business network that provided the foundation of this market sectors growth.

Extranets

The foundation of any business to business system is your *extranet*. This gives you the channel to create secure communications between your intranet, and shared portions of the system that are externalized to your business partner(s). Hence, the term *extranet*.

The extranet will provide a secure gateway for visitors coming in from the outside, and gives them controlled access to the portions of data that they have permission to see, modify or publish. In some cases, the extranet can also be used to

> *Smart quotes*
>
> Recognizing the need for an e-business model is the slam-dunk; finding the *right* model is the challenge.
>
> Brian Gillooly (Editor, *Information Week*)

provide access to legacy systems via a web interface, or by other means. This allows business partners to gain access not just to data that is located on the extranet web, but other internal systems that are important to your business relationships.

Most applications can be delivered via an extranet, and are secure at the application level. This means that the business partner submits a password to gain access to the system. (Obviously, other security schemes can be used, but this is a common one.)

SAMPLE STARTER APPLICATIONS FOR A
BUSINESS-TO-BUSINESS EXTRANET

Technology	Application
Secure electronic mail	Business to business communications
Bulletin board	Subject review and response vehicle, frequently asked questions
Instant messaging	Sales and Customer support
Document Repository	Knowledge Management and customer support
FTP	Customer support, sales support, software development
Mail list server	Broadcast of changes and notifications
Calendar	Scheduling
Data conferencing and chat	Electronic meetings

In addition to electronic mail and secure posting of information some starter applications for an extranet include those listed in the table above.

While these may be typical for your first stage extranet applications, there are no restrictions of how sophisticated your extranet could become.

As you consider issues in the development of your extranet, consider the number one issue: *security*. Visitors coming into the extranet usually deal with sensitive data that is confidential in nature. You should ensure that external business partners only have access to information appropriate for your specific business arrangement.

Until recently, it was difficult to consider creating an extranet without first having an intranet, however this is changing. In 1999, new extranet solutions have emerged that are hosted outside of the company facilities. (These are hosted by application service providers.) If you want to develop an extranet, but want to avoid the hosting and security issues managed by your staff, this is a reasonable alternative. This way you have the benefit of avoiding buying sophisticated security software, as the hosting firm offering the system will provide most of the security tools. However, the net effect is the same for the users.

Virtual private networks

Virtual private networks (VPNs) is another popular method of providing point to point security for business to business networks. By using a VPN you and your partner's businesses can connect to each other in a secure manner, but still have the convenience of the Internet as the wire to transmit the data. This can save thousands of dollars, and allows easy access for your partners that need to collaborate with you.

Smart things
to say about
e-commerce

Virtual private networks

Private networks that allow users to purchase bandwidth and access, often through their Internet connection, without the need to purchase dedicated network cabling or systems.

Internet-based VPNs are becoming a common method of linking remote offices to a common network. The technology used for this is known as *tunneling*. As the name suggests, it provides a way of linking various VPN locations across the Internet while enforcing security using tunneling.

Many large telecommunication companies in the market are re-marketing their excess capacity to VPN providers. You may find this is a good method to acquire additional bandwidth without the need to pay until you use it. As each month passes, this new technology becomes more affordable. Depending where your business is located, this technology may impact the choice of network. By using VPNs for a group of suppliers, and then providing applications that can meet their needs, the concept of a ready-made extranet has become a reality.

You can select software and hosting firms who offer packages that allow groups of businesses to collaborate using ready-made applications from day one. Most of these applications require a sign-up process on the Internet and then you are ready to go. VPNs are a particularly good choice if you are considering supply chain applications, where you need to be connected

Smart things
to say about
e-commerce

Tunneling

A secure mechanism to allow transmission of data across points of access on the Internet.

to a partners network for a longer period, or may need access to multiple applications outside the scope of a simpler collaborative extranet.

Supply chains

Supply chains are a well-established method of linking businesses and their processes together. Many are focused on building, selling and supporting products in national and multi-national chains.

Companies which have successful supply chain and manufacturing systems put themselves ahead of others in the market. Creating this advantage and staying flexible to meet differing market conditions gives these leading companies an edge that is hard to beat.

Firms such as Dell Computer, which have combined their focus on the end customer with a great web delivery strategy, have gone from strength to strength. They build all their products to order, and are currently accumulating these orders at the rate of more than $14 million daily from their e-commerce web site. At the other end of the spectrum, Boeing Aircraft, a leading producer of capital goods has invested heavily to improve its supply chain organization in the past two years.

Businesses use supply chain management software and systems to improve the way their businesses are operating. Typical reasons for purchasing and implementing systems include those set out in the table overleaf.

As more firms' products and services continue to expand at a global level, the need to consider the impact of the Internet and supply chain systems increases. The cost of entering sophisticated supply chains and systems is changing.

REASONS FOR SUPPLY CHAIN MANAGEMENT SYSTEMS

Function	Desired improvement
Inventory management	Cut inventory volume
Manufacturing management	Ensure that products are delivered on time in most efficient manner
	Cut manufacturing cycle times
	Increase revenues
Procurement	Reduction in costs of goods produced
Distribution management	Improved sales and delivery timeframes

Businesses use supply chains to improve their competitive position in the marketplace. Management continues to concern itself with the issues of globalization; competition and meeting the demands of consumers. These issues come high on the list of driving reasons to continue to develop their supply chain and hone its operation. Many companies in the past have focused on various individual aspects of the problem, such as procurement or inventory management. Today the view tends to be much more holistic, with a total review of parties involved in all aspects of the supply chain to create the best potential value and results.

> **Smart things to say about e-commerce**
>
> The Internet is influencing the behavior of supply chain systems and provides a tremendous opportunity for companies to leverage their strengths in ways not possible before.

The Internet has created some significant opportunities for companies to create a virtual supply chain of partners, not only inside their current markets, but also outside. This allows firms to more

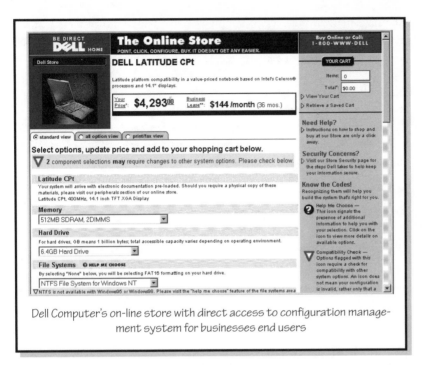

Dell Computer's on-line store with direct access to configuration management system for businesses end users

rapidly develop the support mechanisms and systems to build clear improvements in the way that they are operating in the marketplace.

Smart things to say about e-commerce

Reasons for supply chain management systems:

- Consumers and businesses demand improved service, more choice and lower costs.
- Competition continues to increase.
- More parts and finished goods may have to be shipped to and from different locations around the world.
- Internet and related technologies have a potential huge impact on the rate of change in distribution supply chains and consumer behavior.

By using many of the existing supply chain software and systems that are already in place in the organization, companies can add significant value to their product offerings.

The really interesting aspect of supply chains is that they provide the foundation for so many other opportunities in the business-to-business sector. The relationships, along with optimized systems and methods of procurement, are now giving way to new next generation systems that are morphing themselves into digital marketplaces.

Digital markets

Digital marketplaces are now emerging with many variations on the theme.

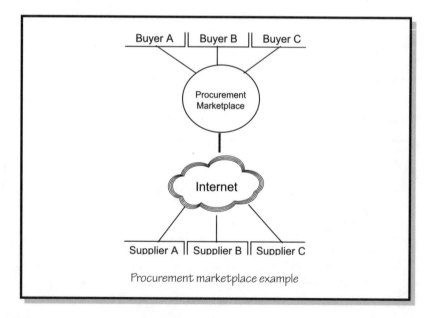

Procurement marketplace example

These will become the foundation of electronic business as we know it. If any of us are lucky enough to predict the winners that make the majority of the predicted trillion dollar market, some extremely good outcomes will result.

Here now things are developing. The traditional brick and mortar companies with excellent supply chains need to optimize them to lock in and expand their partner bases. Ford and GM have both recently taken steps to make this happen, with massive initiatives in procurement and supply chain management.

The procurement marketplace model creates a market to provide products to buyers in a controlled and packaged forum. Many organizations are now looking to this type of model to automate the purchasing of products and services, saving money and optimizing relationships and quality as a result.

Most of the procurement markets today are still based on the catalog model. In this scenario, the product primary benefits are rapid identification of the services that are needed in a pre-approved form. This dramatically reduces the procurement timeframe and costs, and often gives the buyer a wider range of alternative suppliers.

Smart quotes

[Referring to Philips' aim of having about 400 smaller distributors linked electronically by year's end, and all 1,000 on-line by the end of 2000]

By then, you'll do business with us electronically, or you won't do business with us.

Jim Worth, (Director, e-commerce, at Philips Lighting Co.)

Smart things
to say about
e-commerce

About different purchasing and acquisition models:

- The catalog model allows pre-defined offerings, availability and pricing to be packaged for the buyers.
- On-line auctions allow buyers, sellers and traders to interact freely to determine the market price for products, commodities and services.
- Business exchanges are based more on a stock market model, where the price of goods and commodities will vary according to supply, demand and value perceptions at a given time.

Two other models are involved in the business-to-business space today. These are the auction and the exchange. The auction offers the ability of buyers, traders and sellers to interact in a controlled commercial environment. These systems are still very specialized in nature, but extend the pricing and competitive nature of procurement. The auction allows the buyers and sellers to reach agreement

Business-to-business portals and exchanges

Portals for B2B are moving fast. The difference between a portal and an exchange is also starting to become a blurred line.

Today portals provide a wide range of services at an industry, community or individual company level. While we may want to define this more clearly, companies such as Microsoft, General Motors or Ford are large enough to create individual portals that can be bigger than a small industry.

These portals and exchanges can provide a wide range of services including relevant news, information, training, support, products, access to business partners and transaction support.

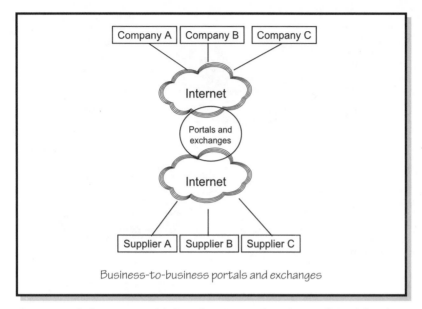

Business-to-business portals and exchanges

Some portals focus on multiple industries, such as VerticalNet. This firm and site is an infomediary, providing relevant information for a wide range of industries.

The strategy for many sites is to build traffic first, and then gradually expand the offering of the site to offer e-commerce products and services over time.

Others take a different approach, focusing on a single industry, such as PlasticsNet.com. This operation is providing a location for information, transactions and potentially huge changes to the way that a very large industry works. (Plastics alone is a $370 billion dollar industry.)

Supporting all of these sites is an increasingly sophisticated range of technologies. After all, it is one thing to post relevant content and articles and

VerticalNet.com offers a home to many industry specific
business-to-business portals

handle a few transactions. It is quite another to provide real-time broker
style trading with complex transactions rules. If you decide that it is your
business to tackle one of these areas, then make sure that you pick a vendor or partner who really knows what they are doing. Most of these systems are non-trivial to build and implement.

Business networks and syndication

The development of a business network for e-commerce is an evolving

PlasticsNet.com, an industry specific business exchange

concept. Business networks differ from Supply Chain networks in several ways.

Supply chain networks often involve products and less services, whereas business networks can include both. Business networks include direct distribution and other partners that have value for the function of the business.

For the successful development of any business network, all aspects of the sales, distribution and support process need to be considered. To ensure

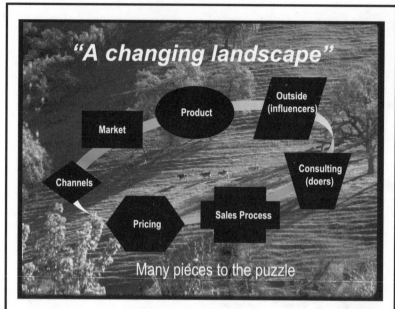

"A changing landscape"

Product

Outside (influencers)

Market

Consulting (doers)

Channels

Pricing

Sales Process

Many pieces to the puzzle

Many variables are involved in the development of a business network

that there is effective distribution of the product or service, it should meet the requirements of the market and those of the distribution channels and consumers.

A useful way to consider this is to visualize these variables in the framework of a distribution ecosystem. As with other ecosystems, plants sur-

Smart things to say about e-commerce

Channels

Distribution channels to provide alternative ways of selling and supporting product instead of selling direct to the consumer.

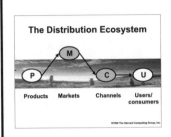

The Distribution Ecosystem

Products   Markets   Channels   Users/consumers

©1999 The Harvard Computing Group, Inc.

Ideal positioning for
distribution strategy

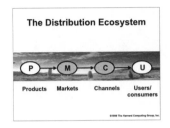

The Distribution Ecosystem

Products   Markets   Channels   Users/consumers

©1999 The Harvard Computing Group, Inc.

Market change has caused a
problem and needs to change again

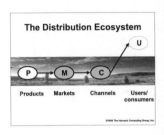

The Distribution Ecosystem

Products   Markets   Channels   Users/consumers

©1999 The Harvard Computing Group, Inc.

Consumer or end user
behavior has changed

Areas that can impact distribution strategy in business networks

vive best when you provide good support for them. When things change, then so do results and the outcome is altered. As you develop your business network, consider how the product should be priced, packaged, distributed, delivered and supported. Developing business networks needs careful thinking and smart moves. For example, by using other channels, the cost of creating effective distribution can be lowered, and the risk associated with a single channel initiative reduced.

One method of building and expanding a business network is to create a group of affiliates organizations. If you have a product that can be sold by

- How should information be passed through the system?
- Are there different types of markets that you will need to address?
- Is the e-commerce strategy intended as the major method of selling, or will there be other channels that will sell the products?
- Is the product deliverable via the Internet, or does it require additional packaging and shipping?

KILLER QUESTIONS

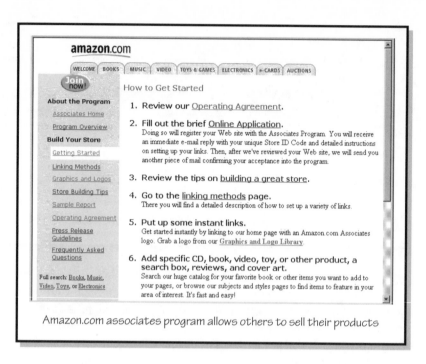

amazon.com

WELCOME | BOOKS | MUSIC | VIDEO | TOYS & GAMES | ELECTRONICS | e-CARDS | AUCTIONS

Join now!

About the Program
Associates Home
Program Overview

Build Your Store
Getting Started
Linking Methods
Graphics and Logos
Store Building Tips
Sample Report
Operating Agreement
Press Release Guidelines
Frequently Asked Questions

Full search: Books, Music, Video, Toys, or Electronics

How to Get Started

1. **Review our** Operating Agreement.

2. **Fill out the brief** Online Application.
   Doing so will register your Web site with the Associates Program. You will receive an immediate e-mail reply with your unique Store ID Code and detailed instructions on setting up your links. Then, after we've reviewed your Web site, we will send you another piece of mail confirming your acceptance into the program.

3. **Review the tips on** building a great store.

4. **Go to the** linking methods **page.**
   There you will find a detailed description of how to set up a variety of links.

5. **Put up some instant links.**
   Get started instantly by linking to our home page with an Amazon.com Associates logo. Grab a logo from our Graphics and Logo Library.

6. **Add specific CD, book, video, toy, or other product, a search box, reviews, and cover art.**
   Search our huge catalog for your favorite book or other items you want to add to your pages, or browse our subjects and styles pages to find items to feature in your area of interest. It's fast and easy!

Amazon.com associates program allows others to sell their products

others, many options are available to increase channel bandwidth and effectiveness.

Amazon.com have created a vast network of business affiliates. They build this by offering associates part of their profit margin resulting from sales or referrals. This type of business network and syndication of products is a very inventive method to gain improved market visibility.

This will all lead to the next stage of development in the market, the syndication of products and content. This is likely to explode over the next twelve months, with products, technology and new distribution strategies that will likely make your jaw drop.

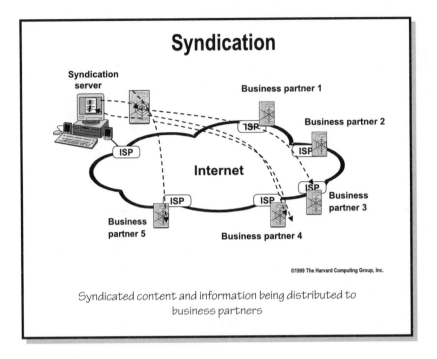

Syndication

Syndication server

Business partner 1

Business partner 2

ISP

ISP

Internet

ISP

ISP

ISP

Business partner 3

Business partner 5

Business partner 4

©1999 The Harvard Computing Group, Inc.

Syndicated content and information being distributed to business partners

Syndication

This next phenomenon allows you to quickly and easily create your own business network, complete with management tools for affiliates and others in their chain of distribution.

Syndication will be successful because it allows the same product to be presented differently, packaged differently, and priced differently for targeted audiences. It will also permit the reuse of content on a major scale, without all of the technical indigestion and work of the early years in web development.

Smart things to say about e-commerce

About syndication:

- Syndicate when you have components that can be used in many different assembly and product configurations.
- Syndicate when you have a product that many people want, but your business partners want to brand it themselves.
- Syndicate when you want to get your products or services located on as many affiliate web sites as possible.
- Syndicate if you have content that can be re-purposed in many ways.
- Syndicate if you have a e-commerce offering that will add value to others in your business network.

By proactively managing affiliates, it will become easy to ensure that you can offer your brand and products to as many web sites as possible, at the same time actually reducing the amount of work involved in the process.

The technology currently on the market to support these functions will allow customized management of content and digital delivery of only the relevant content for that particular member of the business network.

Making them work

Organizations around the globe are using Internet business-to-business technologies in truly productive and astounding ways. From procurement systems, that automate the way that materials and products are purchased, through to sophisticated customer management systems to improve and automate the process.

The categories of systems in the market for business-to-business e-commerce cover a wide range. After all, isn't the customer management sys-

> There has to be an executive sponsor from the top that has the E-business religion. If that person isn't up there saying that the Web is one of the most important things in our business today, you're simply not going to move fast enough.
>
> Phil Gibson (Director, Interactive Marketing, National Semiconductor)

Smart quotes

tem sitting in the corner of the data center providing just as much value as another that is processing orders? You may often only consider e-commerce associated with the money we collect from these systems. However, any productivity improvements that contribute to the bottom line should be considered fair game for e-commerce applications.

Customer management systems

The customer management example is a great way to consider how to really leverage e-commerce solutions. The shortage and expense of qualified IT staff in the North American market has caused many firms to re-think their customer management strategies. Many firms are focused on developing knowledge bases and customer management systems that are Internet based to help deal with the shortfall.

One such firm, who recognized the staffing problem early in their development, was Cisco Systems. They started out early in this process to build a web site that would provide the information that their clients were looking for, particularly for their software products and support. The system provided software updates in downloadable form, with the accompanying documents all via the Internet. Cisco estimates that they have saved themselves over $75 million in staff savings alone, along with the packaging and shipping savings of software products downloaded directly from the web. In 1998, they estimated these savings to be in the order of $250

About customer management systems:

- Use customer management systems to assist in the delivery and recording of business-to-business transactions.
- Create knowledge bases that will allow business partners to get access to information via your extranet.

million. Today, the web deals with more than 70% of their support calls, without additional follow-up required.

Technology firms such as Eclipsys have also benefited from e-commerce solutions based on linking knowledge bases to customer databases. In a bold move this software company made the decision to develop their knowledge management repository for their clients and business partners, and at the same time implement an enterprise Customer Relationship Management system.

While initially they had considered just implementing one of these systems, the dramatic difference in the return on investment from the combination made them make the move effective.

Using the intranet as a foundation for business-to-business

Intranets are a major component of e-business strategies. These systems evolve from departmental needs or enterprise programs driven by organization business goals. Intranets have supplied a way to integrate content, maintain performance, share information, control access, and share data across the organization. Multiple intranet servers, connected by local and wide area networks (LANs and WANs), provide the foundation for distributed Intranets.

Smart things
to say about
e-commerce

About intranets in business to business applications:

- Intranets provide organizations with a flexible way to organize information that can be shared with others in a controlled and expandable way.
- Companies such as MCI WorldCom are using large-scale, distributed intranets to help newly acquired companies become integrated into their operations in months, not years. Distributed intranets can help companies like MCI WorldCom receive a return on their technology investment as high as 500 to 2,000 percent.
- An intranet's technology components are now the raw materials of almost every desktop and support the lowest common denominator of IT standards – the browser, HTTP, and TCP/IP. Nothing on that list scares even the most conservative of IT staffers.

Today, most organizations no longer view intranets as a separate component of their IT strategy, and are moving toward a flexible way of organizing information where the content can be shared with others in a controlled, expandable way. This philosophy provides the foundation for the development of distributed Intranets.

As intranets become richer in content and this content is extended to partners and customers, extranets are born. Many firms develop intranets to improve productivity and increase the speed with which information is delivered to their organization. In environments that have a great need to

- Citigroup has 300,000 US customers banking online with 25,000 being added each week.
- Ed Horowitz, a senior corporate officer at Citigroup says it costs Citigroup $450 a year to service a customer in branches compared with less than $150 on the Web.

SMART VOICES

provide accurate information in timely fashion, an intranet's natural ability to expand has made it the technology of choice.

Intranets often provide the basis for the delivery of information needed by the internal staff, such as an employee telephone directory, human resource policies, support information, or a knowledge base. Extranet access can also be offered to certain intranet-based information, such as support information and the knowledge base. Business needs have been vital to the rapid development of intranet. These business drivers include the need to rapidly adapt to change, distribute information, and improve existing information delivery techniques. Other factors include supporting major strategic initiatives such as knowledge management, e-commerce, or customer relationship management.

Intranets are a relatively low-cost technology and, on top of that, they scale. For example, MCI WorldCom's intranet chief architect, Kevin Crothers, moved his company Intranet from 20,000 to 100,000 users in

Smart things to say about e-commerce

About deploying intranets:

- *employee productivity*
  dynamic information, shorter cycle times, and increased accuracy;
- *cost savings*
  online information distribution versus paper and reduced maintenance costs;
- *knowledge management*
  KM lets you customize information to meet user needs;
- *e-commerce*
  allows customized content, presentation and transactions;
- *customer management improvements*
  integrating business processes with customer relationship management and client-specific information improves business cycles.

less than two years. He estimates that MCI WorldCom has only used a fraction of its intranet system capacity, although the company is currently averaging 1.5 million hits per hour with peaks to 12 million. (MCI WorldCom has an actively logged-on community of 45,000 to 50,000 users.) Crothers says that MCI WorldCom relies on intranet technology to ensure that newly acquired companies are integrated into the operation in months, not years. MCI WorldCom's distributed network includes 500 intranet sites (150 of which are linked under a universal server), 120 IP networks, 1,000 servers, and 70,000 workstations serving roughly 55,000 employees. The staff to develop, deploy, and maintain this large-scale distributed Intranet includes 105 employees and contractors.

Users browse the intranet using either a Microsoft Internet Explorer or Netscape Navigator browser. Intranet applications include an interactive intranet for facilitating IT communications and intranet collaboration, and a Web forum designed to bring together business groups from across the company to analyze how to leverage critical technology tools. Over 600 people from six different sites dialed in to the first real-time collaboration venture, saving the company thousands of dollars in travel costs and downtime.

MCI WorldCom also launched www.wcom.com, an extranet that lets customers access the company's internal customer service information to review their current service and sign up for new programs and services. MCI WorldCom estimates that it has saved more than $45 million in publication costs, employee productivity, and reduced maintenance and development costs since deploying an intranet. For many organizations such as this, the intranet has become a strategic business tool, not just a "nice-to-have" technology option.

The speed and timing of such changes are also important in developing and delivering new work practices. In the large-scale, distributed systems at MCI

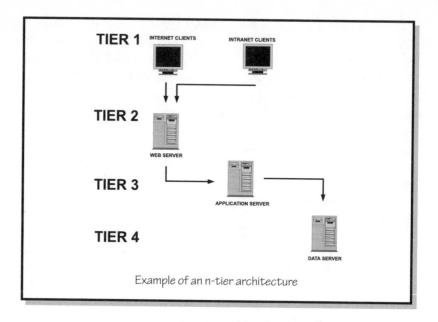

Example of an n-tier architecture

WorldCom, bringing new employees into the newly merged entity happened with incredible speed. One business day after the merger between MCI and WorldCom, the corporate Intranet grew from 22,000 to 110,000 users. All 110,000 users had password access to the enlarged system.

Supply Chain Management

A powerful example of leveraging supply chain management is Cisco Systems. As a global supplier, Cisco has manufacturing plants in many countries; managing this network of factories, suppliers, business partners is critical to the firm. Their supply chain system supported by a powerful e-commerce system has made a huge impact to their bottom line. In their annual report for 1998, the company reported savings totaling $500 million because of these systems.

Cisco has used configuration management and on-line ordering systems since 1997, these tools help their business partners select and configure, get pricing information and conduct business to business e-commerce. With business-to-business sales of more than $5 billion in 1998, Cisco represents one of the largest proponents of e-commerce in industry today.

Internet Commerce

Many business-to-business applications continue to develop in the marketplace. The table below illustrates how some firms have used business to

Industry	Applications	Example
Banking	On-line banking	BankBoston
High tech manufacturing	Supply Chain management	Cisco Systems
Insurance	Policy applications	Intuit
High tech wholesalers and retailers	Procurement and auctions	OnSale.com
Education	Distance learning	NTU
Clothing and retail	Configuration management and e-commerce	Lands' End
Telecommunications	Video-conferencing	A T & T
Publishing	Business to business content, newsfeeds	Ziff Davis
Stock market	Stock trading	Charles Schwab

business to better improve their position in the marketplace, and enhance their business.

The future

Business to business activities remains the largest sector of the market, and shows no signs of stopping. As companies start to really leverage the power of the Internet, and combine the technology with integrated business strategies, powerful results will emerge. The future appears limitless.

Many of the new business-to-business solutions have been made successful by creating new offerings that "traditional" businesses have either ignored, or been too scared to try. Even aircraft carrier size companies can be turned around when there is a desire to do so. Just look at IBM's revival in fortune since Mr. Gerstner's arrival.

Whether your focus is going to be consumer-to-business, or business-to-business, both can improve your organization's work.

You now have to decide how best you can take advantage of the opportunity. There is no shortage of them.

6

Building your own Strategy

The quote below from Charles Schwab may seem a little surprising on first reading. However, when you see how Schwab has *enhanced* their business using technology and new work practices, they have helped to revolutionize an industry. Their strategy has been focused, dramatic, and has shown tremendous market leadership. Schwab's drive as a business

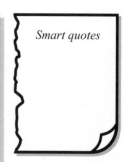

Smart quotes

[On how an e-commerce strategy can influence a business:]

I am often asked how the Internet has changed our business at Charles Schwab. The perhaps surprising answer is: "It really hasn't." Rather than fundamentally changing our business, the Internet has *enhanced* the way we have been operating since I founded the company back in 1971.

Charles R. Schwab (Chairman, the Charles Schwab Corporation), quoted by Tom Siebel, *CyberWars*

leader has fostered an environment that demands both excellence and continuous concern about competitors.

For us mortals out there, understanding how and where to start developing our business strategy for e-commerce often causes consternation, not just new opportunities. As earlier chapters illustrate, just understanding the basics can be a task in itself.

The starting point has to be why do we need a strategy anyway? It turns out that businesses often have both positive and negative reasons for the development of a strategy (see table below).

Surprisingly, many firms develop their strategies because of concern about their position in the market. This worry factor is often high, and while we may not know what we will do, we do know we want to do something.

Development of a strategy often involves complex decisions and changes in the organization, but the starting point has some simple guidelines. Most of these factors rally around money: creating more revenue, reducing costs,

LEADING REASONS DRIVING E-COMMERCE STRATEGY

Positive reasons	Negative reasons
Expand the business	Pressure from competition
Improve marketing	Concern about adoption
Increase competitiveness	Decreasing market share
Desire to take leadership position	Worry

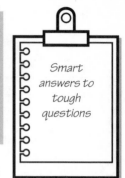

Q: I know that I need do something about e-commerce, but where do I start?

A: Start by looking for the most important reasons (both positive and negative) in the organization why you should develop a strategy. Ask yourself and some close colleagues if you think that the organization would support an e-commerce strategy if they could successfully deal with these issues. Try and look for the leading questions and challenges facing you today.

Smart answers to tough questions

improving margins and staying more competitive. Money makes the world go round, and nowhere is this more true than e-commerce.

However, not every organization's goals are driven purely around return on investment. Organizations such as government and other not-for-profit operations may focus on improving productivity, customer service, reducing administration and supporting their staff and volunteers more effectively. Increasingly these organizations are turning to e-commerce and e-business to effect change.

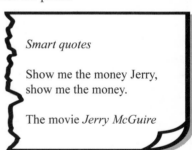

Smart quotes

Show me the money Jerry, show me the money.

The movie *Jerry McGuire*

Types of strategy – your appetite for change

Understanding your organization's appetite for change is a major influence in the development of how your strategy will emerge. Most organizations have a variable appetite for change. These range from voracious to the staid. Determining where you fit into this spectrum can also determine how fast you are able to act.

Certain factors surrounding you determine how much change is acceptable to your organization. Bill Gates, (Chairman of Microsoft Corporation) is an example of someone who, once committed to the Internet, caused his "aircraft carrier" size organization to change and change quickly. Most managers do not have the capability (or resources) to cause such rapid change to occur.

Smart quotes

Never try and teach a pig to sing. It doesn't work and annoys the pig.

Anonymous

E-commerce has a lot in common with high impact strategies. *Too little change can have virtually no impact on the outcome, too much can risk the fundamentals of the business.* As most organizations implement change incrementally, determining the acceptable levels and risk factors influences your strategy development. The following table illustrates examples where differing amounts of change could affect the development of an organization's e-commerce strategy.

Factors such as external regulation, the internal culture, how your organization handles change, whether current strategies are working or failing, all determine the level of e-commerce change your organization can swal-

ILLUSTRATION OF DIFFERING APPETITES FOR E-COMMERCE CHANGE IN THE ORGANIZATION

Organization size	Age	Competitiveness in marketplace	Financial strength	Regulated	Appetite for change
>1,000 staff	10+	Strong	Strong	No	Medium to Low
>1,000 staff	10+	Low	Low	No	High to medium
>1,000 staff	10+	Strong	Strong	Yes	Low
~20 staff	1-2	Moderate	Moderate	No	Very high
~20 staff	10	Good	Good	No	Medium

low. Some great examples of businesses that have enveloped change in a big way are new Internet start-up firms such as Amazon and eBay. They show how a fresh start, without an existing business model to protect, can produce spectacular results.

Where do you think that your organization fits into the "appetite for change" scale? Is your organization going to embrace change or repel it? Keep these factors in mind as we move forward through this chapter.

> The exciting reality is that e-commerce is in its infancy. It is today where the Wright brothers were in aviation. The web is still an infant technology.
>
> Jeff Bezos (Founder of amazon.com)

The ingredients

There are some important ingredients to consider in the development of your e-commerce strategy. These elements have direct input on the development of your strategy, and how much assistance you may need to bring it to market.

These ingredients make up your plan and strategy. Look at them carefully and see how they influence your plans. The diagram overleaf shows that your organization is in the center of these elements. E-commerce has the ability to affect the way that an organization operates in a multi-dimen-

---

About companies who have developed successful e-commerce strategies:

- They are willing to change.
- They have adaptive strategies.
- They understand and focus on partnerships.
- They look at the market differently.

Smart things to say about e-commerce

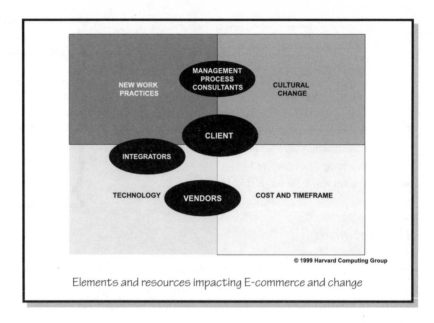

© 1999 Harvard Computing Group

Elements and resources impacting E-commerce and change

sional way. Most e-business strategies have a combination of all of these factors in play.

This is why it is critically important to understand the relationship of these elements to each other. Creating a good balance of these elements will dramatically reduce the risks of failure.

Who to influence and why?

Finding the right sponsors and supporters is a crucial factor for your e-commerce strategy. Your starting point is the identification of these individuals. They are the ones who can *guarantee* the success of your system.

Element and resource	Why they are important
New work practices	Ensure that the program will be supported by new defined and documented methods of working
Cultural change	Many e-commerce systems require significant change in the way that an organization does business. Often these are not always complementary with the current culture and practices.
Technology	The technology provides the infrastructure and components for an e-commerce system. This needs to be developed and deployed to meet the new business, work process and quality goals of the organization.
Cost and timeframe	These are important factors in the development of your strategy and it's supporting plan. Without a project plan, you have no way of measuring progress or success ratios for the program. <u>Do not leave home without one.</u>
Vendors	Suppliers of technology or Internet e-commerce services
Integrators	Professional services companies that will provide you with technology advice and development services
Management work process consultants	Sometimes these services will be available from the Integrator, but often are procured separately. These consultants will provide you with the road map and guide you through the development planning and work process changes critical for success of the system..

Smart things
to say about
e-commerce

Whom to involve in the decision process

- Technical staff (the IT department, MIS, CIO or others influencing this process).
- Operational managers of the organization affected by the system (development, manufacturing, sales, marketing, support, logistics, administrative, HR et al.).
- Executive(s) – Someone at the executive level to champion the cause in the organization, who is committed and will support the project.

Systems are successful because they are supported and used effectively by people. Success starts at the beginning, by involving the involved. Every organization needs the following three groups on board for any program to be successful.

Almost all failed IT projects have some problem with support of the groups named above. Always start by identifying these groups in your organization.

Technology Awareness

SMART VOICES

Build a list of those staff in the three groups critical to the project's success and keep them engaged throughout the project.

In order to make intelligent decisions about e-commerce, some education is required. The place to start is with a basic understanding of the technology and how it has helped other companies. By learning from others' experiences, both positive and negative, a framework of understanding is developed. This will help you understand where to go and why to go there. We call this understanding *technology awareness*. Technology awareness

Smart things
to say about
e-commerce

Why technology awareness is important:

- There are many technology components involved in even a simple e-commerce solution.
- The packaging of these technologies is changing weekly. A full time analyst would be required for most companies to stay current with the components relevant to them.
- E-commerce is changing the landscape of many business deals and operations. As the ultimate weapon in an IT arsenal, learning what others are doing in the market is important.
- Operational managers and executives in particular have very little time to dedicate to the subject of staying current with technology developments.

allows staff to understand not just what the technology can do, but the *relevance* of the technology to your industry and situation.

Building technology awareness in your organization provides a foundation for the development of your strategy. It also starts team building on the project, without which, gaining consensus will be difficult.

This approach can be used to ensure that the project is set on the road to success. Managers and others are much less likely to buy into a program if they don't understand what is going on. Traditional methods of keeping up to date with what technology is out there for the organization do not work well. A more aggressive approach is needed.

SMART VOICES

When building technology awareness in the organization, ensure that each program *clearly illustrates* the relevance of the technology to your business or organization's needs.

- Build a small library of relevant books and articles (see appendices for suggestions).
- Hire an e-commerce consultant to create a dedicated briefing specific for your industry.
- Ask one (or more) of your current suppliers to create a briefing for the relevant staff (understand that the supplier will likely only pitch their products or services, and provide a less than independent view of the world).
- If you have a training department already in place, ask them to organize a short program on the subject.

Developing a Technology Awareness program for the organization can be as simple as attending a seminar or arranging visits from e-commerce consulting operations to outline what is involved in the development of an e-commerce system. A few suggestions are listed in the box above to start the ball rolling.

The most important goal of this program is to demystify the complex questions and issues surrounding e-commerce, allowing staff to begin thinking in an open and exciting way about how to use the technology.

Looking for opportunities in the organization

One of the wonderful aspects of an e-commerce project is looking for

Smart
answers to
tough
questions

Q: How long should technology awareness take?
A: Dependent on the size of your operation, it could take a couple of days, or it may take several weeks. As with many of these issues of change in the organization, getting people to the table can take much longer. However, without some form of technology awareness program in place, buying decisions can take many months.

SMART VOICES

As you scour the organization for opportunities to apply e-commerce, start at the top. Pick the top six things the organization is trying to achieve or change as your starting point. It will *almost ensure* executive support.

places to apply it. There are so many opportunities waiting for organizations to use e-commerce that finding them is usually not the problem. Deciding which you are going to act on is often a bigger deal.

I personally like to start with the six most important items on the company or organization agenda.

Once identified, you have already achieved one of the most important elements for success with your project: *the support of your executives.* By picking the leading problems/goals facing the company, and looking for ways e-commerce is likely to help, you are already on the right road. Taking this approach will also avoid being sidetracked by technology driven or individual agendas. The business requirements are driving the need.

Smart things to do
Stages in opportunity development for e-commerce

1. Look for opportunities that support the primary business goals e.g. improve customer support:

   - increase sales and client base;

   - shorten product development timelines;

   - reduce inventory;

- expand partnership network; and

- reduce publishing costs.

2. Map the opportunities to individual departments and functions:

   - describe how e-commerce might help;

   - gain agreement with department members; and

   - rate the opportunities against business goals;

3. Review the opportunities with the executive(s):

   - begin to quantify the process; and

   - illustrate the opportunities and relevance to the business.

On reaching this stage, you then begin the process of mapping them together in an e-commerce opportunity framework. This becomes the building block for the development of your whole strategy.

The table below shows how an e-commerce opportunity is then mapped to different opportunities to support these goals.

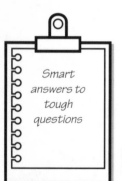

Smart
answers to
tough
questions

Q: Who should I ask for help with my strategy?
A: Start by talking to your customers. Understanding what they want and how they would like to have it delivered provides invaluable insight, buy-in and input to your e-commerce system.

EXAMPLE OF E-COMMERCE OPPORTUNITY FRAMEWORK

E-commerce opportunity	How and where to leverage
Improve customer support	Web based customer management systems, knowledge bases, on-line information delivery, externalization of current internal customer support information, improved work practices at help-desk level.
Increase sales and client base	Web based marketing, one-to-one marketing, personalization, interactive configuration management through the web, secure transactions for purchases via the web.
Reduce publishing costs	Provide information in customized form via the web, generate PDF files for information delivery, use document management technology to distribute appropriate information to parties in electronic form, reduce mail and packaging costs.

Once you have the e-commerce opportunity elements identified, review the document with other relevant staff. As this occurs, your strategy will start to take shape and you will start to gain support for the next stages.

Develop an e-commerce opportunity framework. This includes the opportunity and a basic description of what e-commerce technology and other changes needed to support it.

Smart things to say about e-commerce

Gaining support for your ideas

As ideas start to become quantified, you will start the process of selling them internally. Avoid selling of these ideas as an individual crusade. E-commerce systems, even the simplest ones, have many attributes that generate results, both positive and negative.

As most e-commerce systems require many areas of the organization to participate in complex ways, it is extremely important not to oversimplify the requirements just to gain early support in the process.

We can now review how each of these components comes together. As the diagram below illustrates, business goals, technology, new work processes and the final system have to work together in unison. This unification is an important factor to understand for everyone involved in the decision making process.

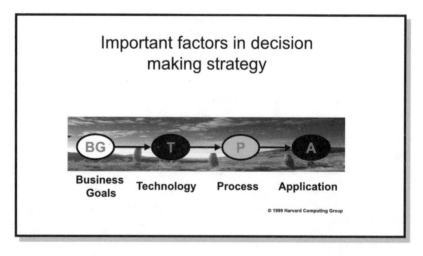

Important factors in decision making strategy

BG → T → P → A

Business Goals   Technology   Process   Application

© 1999 Harvard Computing Group

As your ideas are documented and have gained support from your sphere of influence, then you are then ready to start selling them internally. Some good examples of ways to make this happen are given in the box below.

Checkpoint

At this stage, you should have achieved the following:

- identified the appetite for change inside the organization and built your strategy around something that will fly;

- achieved some reasonable level of technology awareness within the working group of the relevant technology and how others are using it;

- have documented several potential areas in the organization that can use e-commerce effectively to support organization and departmental goals; and

- started to communicate these ideas through the organization.

> *Smart things to say about e-commerce*
>
> Involve groups around the organization early in the process. The later that you do this, the greater the effort will be required to gain buy-in and acceptance for the project.

About selling your ideas internally:

- lunch time briefings (these can be open and informal, and can involve operational managers, execs and others that you are soliciting input);
- departmental and organization-wide meetings to discuss the potential of the technology and where it can be applied;
- posting on the company Intranet (if you have one) in discussion group areas; and
- company newsletters and email to outline strategy and gain feedback.

> *Smart things to say about e-commerce*

Building the business case

Now you have opportunities identified with at least some general support in the organization. The next step is to quantify the potential outcome, or build a business case to support the initiative.

This business case can be as simple as a few bullet slides and a spreadsheet, but is a necessary step to building effective solutions. E-commerce applications often provide very high return on investment, many produc-

---

EXAMPLES OF FACTORS TO BE CONSIDERED IN THE DEVELOPMENT OF THE E-COMMERCE BUSINESS CASE

Business needs	Incremental costs	Soft benefits	Hard benefits
Increased sales	Hardware and software costs	Improved competitiveness	Increased sales
New product	Consulting costs (internal/external)	Customer satisfaction	Shorter sales cycles
Greater market penetration	Marketing and promotion	Better access to information	Improved margins
New business initiatives	Hosting and Internet access costs	Improved corporate image	Reduced costs
	Training and implementation	Increased staff satisfaction	

Source: Harvard Computing Group 1999

ing returns in the range of 500–2,000% or more, successful ones creating tremendous value for the business as a whole.

Many models exist to develop a solid business case, but most require clear measurement of expected outcomes from the system implementation. Discussion groups and workshops are often used to gain consensus and agreement in determining the outcome of e-commerce systems.

The process starts with the information you have captured so far, and integrating it into a format that can clearly show the business needs, costs and benefits associated with the project.

In general hard benefits can and should be measured in budgetary impact to the organization. In other words; real money. Other benefits that have a good effect on the operation can be considered soft, but not measurable in financial terms. When quantifying savings and potential outcomes I recommend that you are conservative on savings and aggressive on costs.

> *Smart things to say about e-commerce*
>
> When estimating costs and benefits be *conservative on savings and aggressive on costs.*

Capturing the information

Now we come to the nasty part, capturing the information. To develop a business case for any major technology space, but particularly e-commerce, you must be ready to break down some doors. Keep the following working groups discussed earlier involved in the process:

- the appropriate executives that could support your ideas

- operations managers who could support your ideas

- IT staff and management who could support your ideas.

Smart things to say about e-commerce

Creating decision-making forums for e-commerce strategies:

- Set up a workshop forum sponsored by one of the executives to discuss the potential opportunity.
- Use any internal change management, IT work process team or CIO/IT support team that has expertise to help develop the business case.
- Hire an external consulting group that can facilitate the business case development.

So many projects go south (not good), because they do not have these groups involved in the process. Pulling these groups together in a common framework is another trick that you perform. Here are some ideas for making it happen:

However you decide to facilitate the development of your business case, the outcomes that you need from this process include:

- impact on the organization

- cost analysis

- savings

- outline of technology plan

- new work practices/processes

- agreement that can be "burned into" a budget.

When developing an e-commerce strategy, do not:

- underestimate the amount of change required in the organization for the solution to work
- forget to look at how your competitors and others in the market have evolved their solutions
- build a strategy that is not based around core business or organizational goals
- try and "boil the ocean" by trying to include everything in the first go around
- undertake little or no research on the impact of change
- try and sell the solution by underestimating costs
- focus on the wrong elements of e-commerce
- forget to factor change management into the program
- sell the system internally without a supporting business case
- hope that the new business practices will start when the new system starts
- become enamored with the technology alone – it should support a business need.

Smart things to say about e-commerce

Impact on the organization

Determining how your organization is going to use e-commerce technology remains the most important and difficult part of defining your strategy. This multi-faceted nature of electronic commerce presents us with many alternatives. Determining exactly which mixture is right for you requires serious review, as decisions made about e-commerce (and ones not made) will likely affect the organization for years ahead. Consider the variables discussed earlier in this chapter; appetite for change, risk aversion, state of the current operation, competition and financial stability. All of these will change the geography of your e-commerce landscape. We can now turn to look at these variables and package them together to determine the positive (and some negative) outcomes from your strategy.

E-COMMERCE FACTORS FOR THE DEVELOPMENT OF THE BUSINESS CASE

E-commerce factors and components

People	Influencers	The client (consumer)	Client (business to business)	Advertisers	Internal staff
Processes	Sales process	Market feedback	Advertising and promotion	Customer support	Maintenance of site
Content	The product	The service	Marketing and catalog information	Legal agreements and contracts	Corporate information
Technology	Infrastructure and development platforms	Security	Content management	Multi-language support	Hosting and access
Transactions	Purchase	Electronic funds transfer (payment)	Fulfillment	Shipping	Taxation

The table above illustrates example components and factors that affect your strategy development. It is little wonder we all need some help in putting together successful systems.

Cost analysis

As you understand the opportunities and the applications identified your next objective is to measure the savings. Start by measuring these at two points in the process. Firstly with the tasks in your current environment, and then comparing these with the expenses after the system has been put in place.

By now, you are probably getting the picture. The devil is in the details of these estimates. I would advise that you be conservative with the savings estimates, after all you may be responsible for making them happen. The good news is there are so many opportunities for improvement (in most organizations) for e-commerce that finding these improvements is not nearly as hard as you might think.

Once you have the savings element under control, the time to consider the cost side of the equation has come. Again, these calculations do not need to be Byzantine, but they must be believable and relevant to your operation's accounting and procurement rules.

Smart quotes

EDI (the standard in electronic commerce) is not a choice. It is the inevitable way business will be done.

MIT, *Presence Program*, 1990

Estimating costs

Having identified your applications and outlined how they will be used, we then estimate the costs of building, implementing, and supporting them. To build a good estimate, start with all of the components. The table overleaf shows some examples of ones that you should factor into the system.

Identification of the components and evaluating the incremental staff resources provide the framework for the estimate. Wherever possible try and use existing systems or platforms as this will keep maintenance costs down, and speed start up timeframes.

Your next step is to estimate the cost of the technology infrastructure that will support the applications. Ideally, your goal will be to identify a common

Cost estimate components	
Hardware	Servers, desktop, network, routers, gateways
Software	Servers, desktop, network. one-time purchases and development costs
Development and Implementation	One-time consulting, database population, conversion, training, and testing costs
Support (maintenance)	Annual system administration, hosting services, support, and maintenance costs

infrastructure for all applications. This is because an infrastructure that supports many applications can lower costs considerably.

Calculating return on investment (ROI)

Calculating the return on investment is, in many ways, the easy part. Now you have identified better methods of working, projected savings and what

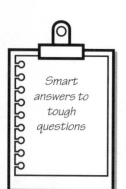

Smart answers to tough questions

Q: How can I reduce additional costs introducing e-commerce systems into the organization?

A: One way is to re-use existing infrastructure and systems that are already in place. It is likely that you already have standards in place for web servers, databases, browsers and application development tools. If you can use these tools in your solutions, the adoption and maintenance costs of the system will be greatly reduced.

they will cost, you merely need to put the numbers together. Often the most difficult aspect of calculating the ROI is putting the numbers together in a way that meets your own organization's financial and budget policies. For example, payback periods may vary depending upon how capital purchases are treated and amortized in the organization. In addition, the organization's cash flow may require the cost of borrowing money to be included in the equation. Talk to accounting and other organizations responsible for procurement and how capital purchases are handled. They should be able to give you some guidelines to help in this matter.

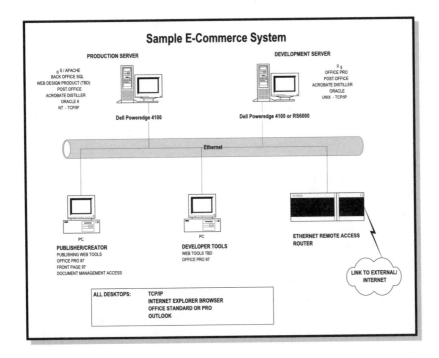

The technology plan

Some form of technology plan should be included in the business plan. This does not have to be a detailed application specification but should reflect the components that are part of the solution. This can be as simple as a diagrammatic view of the system, as shown previously. However, it should illustrate that the basic components have been identified and how they will work in the system.

New work practices and business processes

Determining the new work practices and business processes associated with the system is very important. You may have simple work process requirements such as defining site and product pricing updates, or they may be more complex, such as defining business to business protocols and work processes for distribution and development partners. Part of the successful definition of the business case is to review these procedures when determining the business case. What is the use of spending thousands of dollars on an e-commerce web site, but having no method to deliver the goods? Believe me it has been done before. Many new work process factors may have little to do with the transaction itself, but can speed the decision making process, or accelerate sales cycles. E-commerce will provide you with the opportunity to improve and cement business partnerships, and develop new relationships by offering improved service and support.

Many business processes are linked to what are known as self-service or personalization applications (discussed earlier in Chapter 4). These are designed to provide information directly to the person who needs it without further intervention. Customer Support applications have become very popular for these technologies, particularly when they are combined with a supporting knowledge base providing information to customers as they need it.

Business processes cannot be ignored. If they are, e-commerce applications may actually increase costs and provide little or no benefit to anyone involved. Just as strategy will provide drivers for change, new business processes must be developed to support it.

Defining new business processes is beyond the scope of this book, however they need to be carefully examined in any e-commerce solution. The web allows us to rethink the way that we can do business together, with our business partner and consumers. If we do not take advantage of it, many opportunities may be left "on the table".

Gaining agreement and phased approach

By now, you will have gained agreement from the others comprising your new e-commerce team. You will have identified many opportunities and applications that could make a difference to your organization. As you reach this stage, another prioritization should take place. You can then take a phased approach to the project, ensuring that the project and scope will be successful.

To build a phased approach:

- select several tasks and applications that are high value and easy to implement;

- pick some high visibility items that ensure that the team will have success and start working effectively together; and

- break the project into the following time-lines 0–3 months, 3–6 months, greater than 6 months.

Smart things to say about e-commerce

About developing an e-commerce strategy:

- Ensure that you have management support for the project.
- Involve the appropriate parties.
- Make sure that all involved have a good understanding of the technology, and the way the operation may have to change to support it.
- Focus on high return, high profile opportunities.
- Think out-of-the-box in reviewing alternatives.
- Prioritize alternatives based on business or organizational goals.
- Develop and agree a budget (by whatever means).
- Document the business case.
- Develop a phased approach.

Most e-commerce business decisions are being made in Internet time. However, making your move does not necessarily mean high risk and long timeframes. A careful choice of strategy and plan can allow to you to move quickly and in the right direction. As your strategy begins to fall into place, determining the next stage of how to make this happen becomes the challenge.

7

Making it Happen – Doing E-commerce

Recently, I had a meeting with a financier of Internet startup firms. This individual normally takes great care to ensure that he has relevant research information about the company, the market and how the firm is going to be successful. All of this is factored into his decision-making process. In reviewing a business plan for a potential investment, he asked me whether it was necessary to conduct market research for the firm in question. His argument was simple, if the firm can do what they say and can sign up 10,000 users in 3 months, with a powerful business argument, who cares about targeting the marketplace. As Nike might say, "Just do it!" Now, this is not to say that recommendations from previous chapters are not relevant, but it does show that we face comparisons on the web that change our method of thinking. One thing is for sure, at some point we have to go for it. Once we reach this point, we have to make some decisions. The first one is how much help from the outside do I need?

Internal or external resources

A decision you will have to make early in the process will be *who is going to make it happen.* As e-commerce systems require a significant blend of business, technology and work process change, it is likely that you will need some outside help. Several factors will determine how much of your individual project should include external resources. These will change according to the importance of particular functions to the success of the system, and how much control your organization wants to have over them. In many financial applications for example, companies want to have total control over the computer systems for a variety of regulatory, security and business process reasons. However, other companies may take advantage of the wholesale outsourcing of their projects.

Smart things
to say about e-commerce

NIH
Not invented here

We'll start this process by reviewing various aspects of the project and determine which elements are targets for external support or assistance. The following table illustrates some of the elements and how resources could be allocated in a typical project.

The examples in the table below reveal where resources could be allocated in this model. As recently as 1998, most complex systems involved a tremendous amount of complex programming in their development. Today there is a great opportunity to reduce the amount of programming required in the development and even the hosting of the project. Before deciding to "become your own expert" in each one of these areas, review the table below which illustrates how many of these functions can be outsourced today.

The previous chapter dealt with many of the issues in the development of the strategy and how to build the business case. Now you have to make the decisions that are critical to the success of the systems. Selecting which partners to work with is the starting gate of this process.

TABLE ILLUSTRATING DIFFERENT DIVISIONS OF LABOR WHEN MAKING INTERNAL VERSUS EXTERNAL DECISIONS

Technology awareness	Business requirements	Application specification	Project management	Development	Training	Help desk	Support	Administration
Significant outsourcing of the development and support of the e-commerce system								
Internal	Internal	Complete outsourcing of all technical and support functions						
No outsourcing of services, just limited assistance in the definition and selection of technology components								
External	Internal resources							
Mixture of internal and external resources for various stages of the project								
External	External	External	External	Internal	External	Internal	Internal	Internal

---

About external versus internal resources:

- Do I have the resources to define the system requirements and the work process needs?
- Has my organization the appropriate development resources and experience to build our e-commerce systems?
- How much of our existing systems would be used in the development or deployment of an e-commerce solution?
- How will the content be maintained and updated?
- Who will administer and control the system after it is installed?
- Do we have existing products that could provide the foundation of a new system?

Smart things to say about e-commerce

Selecting partners

Finding and picking the right partners will be the most important decisions you make in the entire process. The following guidelines that can help you identify what to look for in successful partners, both in the selection of the technology vendors and consultants that you hire to assist with the implementation.

FACTORS FOR SELECTING PARTNERS FOR E-COMMERCE INITIATIVES

Selection issue	Areas of concern						
Platform support	Operating system	Network operating standard	Compliance with standards	Web support	Thin client	NPR - no programming required	Use and compatibility with leading programming systems
Financial viability	Is e-commerce a core business?	Well funded	Profitable				
Quality	References	Reliability of systems	Release schedules	Time for critical fixes	Escalation procedures	Test drive the help desk	Knowledge Base
Price	Licensing scheme	Cost per seat	Maintenance cost	Server base pricing	Web pricing	Partner program	
Performance	Number of transactions	Impact on desktop	Network performance	Remote access	Database engine	Overhead	Scalability
Business practices	Integrity	Pricing policies	Guarantees	References	Attentiveness	Quality of staff	Responsiveness
Support	Help desk	Standard support contracts	Response times	Consulting support	Training	Local offices	
Maintenance	Cost of administration	Software distribution	Fixes policy and guarantee period	Cost of maintenance, help desk, fixes, updates	Frequency of updates		

By using a matrix such as the one shown above, it is easy to start rating the companies based on factors that are important to you.

Platform support

Platforms are the software and hardware products that your system will be developed. Ensuring that both internal and external development staff are familiar with your platform plans in the organization could be an expensive decision. This will influence the results you obtain, both in time and performance.

If your organization already has standards in place, it makes sense to use them as the baseline for new systems technology. For example if a particular web server or database is available and supported in your organization, then pick companies that have products and staff familiar with them. Many organizations will tout their services as being "open", however this often means that they will use whatever you want, but may be learning these products for the first time on your "dollar". This not only increases costs, but will also compromise timeframes and the quality of the results. It usually makes sense to do business with an organization that already has skills in a particular area, even if they are not as "open" as some other firms.

Financial viability

Avoid doing business with companies that are not financially sound. Sounds like simple advice doesn't it? However, in the Internet space, many products are developed and brought to market by innovative start-ups that can cut months off a systems development timeline and reduce maintenance costs. (Many content management systems are in this category, with few vendors in the market for more than 24 months.) Careful consideration should be given to understanding the financial backing of companies in this space, sometimes the "new kid on the block" can be the innovative one, shaving time and money from large system procurements.

Quality

Quality of product and services remains an important decision point for doing business with a company. As a significant amount of your firm's business may be tied to the success of this system, paying attention to quality is paramount. In particular among product companies, examine references (in similar applications if possible), release schedules (notoriously subject to slippage even on the Internet), talk to user groups or communities if possible. Many companies now have a great deal of customer support materials and services available on-line. Look at their bulletin boards, FAQ databases, knowledge bases and other support programs provided to help their clients after systems have been installed and supported. You can use the Internet to get the skinny on these firms.

Pricing

Everyone is sensitive to price when developing a new system. Pricing dynamics and the Internet are a continuously changing phenomenon. In general, software is still sold using server based pricing, with a license charge according to the number of users of the system. (There are some variations to this model, but in the main, this continues to be a common practice.) Some firms now will offer combined services, where the software, maintenance and the hosting of the system are included in the price. (This will vary according to the amount of traffic, users or transactions of the system.)

Price comparisons have to take into account various factors that affect each other in e-commerce pricing. These can be complex, nevertheless it is

Smart things to say about e-commerce

When considering price comparisons:

- Incremental software costs
  - product costs
  - annual maintenance costs
  - staffing costs for internal support
- Development and deployment costs
  - timeframe
  - type of contract (fixed price, time and materials)
  - maintenance costs
  - hosting

an important exercise. With many Internet offerings, firms want to engage you with their platform at the entry price, but then expand their offerings (read revenue) as your system needs to grow. This is not necessarily a bad thing, but be sure to compare apples with apples at this stage of your procurement.

Performance and scalability

Even the best designed systems fail. The performance of your e-commerce solution will be criteria for early success or failure of the project. It is amazing how little patience Internet users have today for systems that have long load times, meager performance or other factors that make the experience bad. If your server is out of action when the consumer or client wants to use it, then no amount of "under construction" signs will help you out. Knowing the habits of Internet consumers successful companies understand the importance of making their experience a fulfilling and pleasant one. Performance is crucial to getting this right.

Smart quotes

The Net is doubling in size every two and a half years. In two years it will be ten times larger than the telephone network.

Larry Roberts (designer of ARPAnet infrastructure)

Part of this process is picking a system and architecture that is scalable, and can be expanded quickly and easily. Fortunately, most systems are now built on n-tier architectures that will provide you both scalability and dramatic improvements in performance, with little changes to the architecture. Companies in the financial services and the on-line auction business are good examples of systems that have been implemented with this scalability factor in mind. (When one of these systems fails for whatever reason, it becomes national news.)

Business practices

Your e-commerce partners are likely to be around for a while, therefore making sure that you get on well with each other becomes an important factor in the relationship. Unlike other technologies, you can expect to see a lot of change occurring in the systems as they are developed and deployed. For this reason, it is even more important that flexibility, trust and understanding are part of the relationship. When changes are required to your e-commerce systems, they are usually required quickly. Therefore building relationships with partners that can provide speedy responses to rapidly changing market conditions is very important. As many systems require a deep and confidential knowledge of your business operations and strategy, having partners that you can truly trust in more than just the legal sense is imperative.

Support

You will need support from Internet-based partners at various stages of the development, deployment and operation of your system. This can come in various forms, including:

- help desk

- training and technology transfer

- on-site support

- client support.

Depending on the amount of support that you plan to have outside the company, there are different business models to meet your support needs. You might decide to outsource all but the most essential aspects of the system, or you may want everything in your control and therefore use internal staff.

When you plan to use vendors and integrators, consider their cycle times and escalation procedures to ensure they meet your needs. As it is likely that you will have several vendors, and perhaps one or two consulting operations assisting with the system, keep the support criteria built to standards that meet your business needs. Otherwise there could be some significant consequences. (For example if one vendor commits to a four-hour response on critical problems, and another's response is 24, the 24-hour response becomes the new low point for critical support.)

Maintenance

Maintaining your e-commerce system has many facets. Some of the more obvious ones have already been reviewed earlier. Other areas that you should consider include:

- software updates and administration of the system

- updates and delivery of changes to users of the system

- maintaining content, policy and pricing.

The first two issues are ones that all system administrators have to deal with, the third provides a great opportunity for flexibility and cost reduction.

If a vendor or integrator requires their own staff to make changes to the system and its content as the *only* way of updating the system, *beware*. Many organizations have locked themselves into systems that are difficult to change, update and modify. These relationships cause problems, they are based on an old model of content maintenance and *should be avoided*. You may recognize some of the problems. This type of system is based on an old funnel for information delivery and publishing processes. Here the

Smart things to say about e-commerce

About content maintenance:

- Make sure that the users responsible for the content on your web site can modify it simply and locally from their computer.
- Do not allow development business partners to take over the maintenance of your web content.

system is based on paper based publishing and information release. This model is redundant in the Internet world. Smart users will drive the content maintenance back to the desktop of the individual responsible for the material. These users should have the ability to change this "anywhere in the world". (This type of distributed maintenance is critical to keeping content fresh.)

Cost of ownership

By developing a cost model that reflects these various decision points, and using the examples in Chapter 6, you can develop a summary of costs to deliver to the decision-makers.

As part of this exercise, illustrate why they will have an ongoing beneficial effect on cost of ownership.

- It will help you understand the difference between offerings from various vendors and suppliers.

- Ongoing training and support costs should be compared with different strategies. For example comparing outsourcing versus internal support of the system.

About understanding your existing tools:

- web servers in use
- web development and authoring tools used for existing Internet solutions
- database products and standards
- communication tools and protocols
- electronic mail and messaging standards.

Integration with the existing Internet infrastructure

A smart place to determine the road ahead is to review exactly what you have in place right now. This may seem like a complex task, particularly if you are not a "techie" familiar with all the vagaries of this world. However, even a simple checklist of items to look for when determining the technical strategy can help.

The short list in the box above provides an excellent starting point for the development of new systems. Most IT organizations will have some preferences and standards in place, even in the smallest operations. By understanding what is already in place, additional costs and duplication of systems can be reduced. You will also be blessed with support from internal IT groups by bringing them into the picture early.

E-commerce systems also introduce many new components. These include e-commerce application servers, transaction servers and sophisticated web analysis tools.

By understanding these integration requirements early in the process also allows for a more co-ordinated project management process. A great deal of success is usually dependent on the support and assistance from the internal IT department.

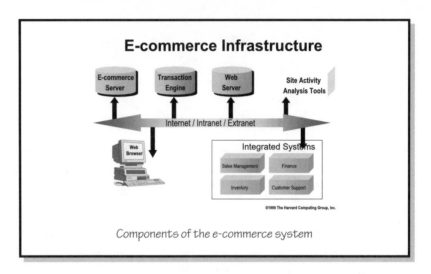

Components of the e-commerce system

Content management and its role in electronic business

Content management and content are words regularly misunderstood in the Internet space. In the early stages of web development most content was funneled and delivered to the webmaster. The webmaster became the center of the world for the development, administration, support and content management of the site. This model has failed miserably. It has caused enormous frustration inside organizations centered around their ability to make changes occur in a timely manner for web site information. In addition to causing difficulty for the maintenance of the site, it also caused burnout to occur with webmasters who suddenly became policy makers, editors, spell checkers and chief arbitrators of what was or was not done.

Smart things
to say about e-commerce

Content
The stuff of the Internet site.

This problem arose because the web was initially viewed as a giant publishing system. However, the issue of how the content was main-

Factors affecting content management:

- interactive content
- distributed information
- customized content.

Smart things to say about e-commerce

tained was overlooked. These problems were also exasperated by the early stage of web development tools. Essentially the market was concentrating on individual authoring tools (such as FrontPage, PageMill, HotDog and others).

The early versions of these tools put the power of HTML authoring in the hands of individuals, but didn't work well in the workgroup scenarios. In addition, staff that owned the content and needed to change it did not have the tools they needed. Hence the bottleneck.

Today, thankfully there are many tools to address this issue. While there is still a need for webmasters to have control over how content is published and managed, (at least from the technical viewpoint), there is little need for them to be involved in the change management process associated with content and how it will be presented. Ideally, this should be driven back to the authors and reviewers associated with this process.

Automated content management systems

Automated content management tools are the answer to the updating and publishing web content. They are now abundantly available in the marketplace and can be tightly integrated into an e-commerce system from the beginning.

Smart things to say about e-commerce

Smart things
to say about
e-commerce

Business impact of content management:

- improved customer relationships
- improved sales and support cycles.

Many organizations have encounted significant problems maintaining their web-based systems. Content management has rapidly become a major issue for many firms to deal with the appropriate maintenance and effectiveness of their web sites.

Content management systems are built specifically to improve the way your operations interact with, and control web-based applications. They are usually selected when three factors are present in the organization's Internet strategy, these are: interactive content, distributed information and customized content.

When to use them

Content management system purchases are often driven by the need for electronic business or e-commerce. Applications include catalogs and product information sites, business to business applications, self-service and customer service applications. These applications usually require careful control and presentation of information providing the most value to the target consumer. At the same time, also require close management of the update, release, and approval processes for the information on the site.

Customers who use content management systems want control and speed. They want quality and customization of both content and appearance. Fortunately, with the modular nature of many content management systems, it is possible to have it all. Content management systems provide the

Typical content management applications:

- catalogs
- personalized publishing applications
- intranets.

Smart things to say about e-commerce

business controls to manage the data presentation; enable distributed updating; make posting new changes fast yet customized.

Content management systems provide a framework to control information. They link the authoring, approval, editing and the release (web publishing) processes. Typically, the sorts of problems that are solved by content management systems include:

- control of updates (in the hands of the content approver, not just the webmaster)

- interactive content which keeps the web site fresh and relevant

- support of the business needs of the operation by providing control over the customization of content for many applications and users.

Options

One choice that many organizations are faced with today is to decide whether to go with a document, publishing or business oriented system. For some applications the choice may not make a difference, where others will clearly benefit from a particular selection. The table overleaf illustrates some examples to help you decide.

Customer application	Application characteristics	Best suited system
Technical publishing, database publishing, knowledge management applications	High volume electronic document applications. Built-in sophisticated information retrieval and PDF generation	Document oriented content management
Catalogs, business to business applications, supply chain and distribution applications	Customization of content and presentation can be controlled interactively. Business rules can be developed and modified easily. High level of personalization	Business oriented content management
Commercial publishing, electronic magazines and personalized content	Customized content can can be presented in many many different forms and formats	Publishing oriented content management

Legacy systems

Although the term has become a little abused in recent years, a legacy system is generally described as an existing computer system that is providing computing support for some part of the business. These systems are often considered older in nature, but often provide some strategic function to the business. Examples include:

- inventory management systems

- manufacturing resource planning systems (MRP)

- enterprise resource planning (ERP)

- sales automation systems

- help desk systems

It is interesting that we now consider certain client/server applications as legacy systems. As legacy systems often have very important information and functions to the organzation, they can be a great resource of information to assist with the building of e-commerce systems. Some examples are given in the table below.

EXAMPLES OF LEGACY SYSTEMS AND HOW THEY CAN BE USED IN E-COMMERCE SOLUTIONS	
Legacy system	Application
Sales automation	Client information base for new e-commerce activities
Inventory management system	Ability to externalize this information to partners and end user clients as part of an Extranet solution
Customer help desk system	Could be used as a browser based interface to an Internet customer management system
MRP (manufacturing resource planning)	Access to the MRP system can allow clients to place order on-line and get information on delivery timelines for special orders

Smart things
to say about
e-commerce

About legacy systems

- Look for databases that can provide continuity with your e-commerce requirements.
- Review departmental databases (marketing, sales, customer support) that have potentially useful seed information for your project.
- Investigate major transaction and business critical databases and systems as part of your plan. Excluding them could cause significant reductions in productivity in future stages of the e-commerce plan.

International considerations

By now, most companies have implemented a presence on the web. Many smart companies and organizations decided to use the web for its capability to go worldwide with their message and product. However, the global nature of the web can also prohibit firms from making the "big move" to international e-commerce. Careful decisions have to be taken before putting US price lists out there for the world to see.

To achieve accelerated sales cycles, potential clients have to see more information in order to make decisions quickly. Meanwhile, corporate concerns about comparative shopping and the public broadcast of previously "private" information, can all gnaw at the current culture of the organization.

These issues and more come to the fore when considering international e-commerce solutions. Determining the timing and methods to implement a program that will be successful can be a daunting task. The web can be a short cut, but there is a huge difference in an "informational site", and using the web as an integrated part of a company's international business.

The road to success may be paved in part, but there are also some road repairs that can make the journey hazardous.

The fundamentals

You will need to consider several factors influencing the development of an international strategy. These factors are often examined separately, but for a successful implementation should be part of a common framework.

One reason why it takes companies time to make this move, is the widespread impact to the organization, clients and distribution systems. Reviewing international e-commerce as either technology or as a better way

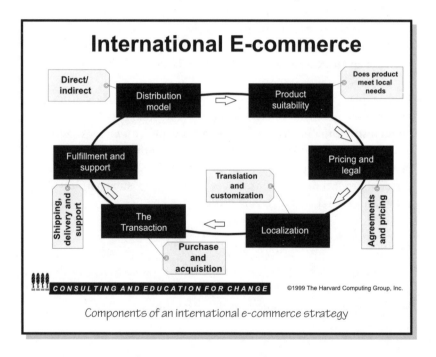

Components of an international e-commerce strategy

of doing business can lead to failure. Successful implementations consider both the business and technology factors as one.

Determining the business model

An international e-commerce strategy can change how a company is doing business in dramatic ways. Understanding the requirements for such a change needs careful consideration. Ensuring that this effect is dramatic in improvement and not traumatic to others is essential for success.

Usually one of three scenarios forms the basis of the business model:

- a new international business on the web;

- changing an existing international direct sales business model; and

- changing an existing international indirect sales business model.

As the table opposite indicates, some major issues have to be considered in the development of this strategy. For companies that already have international distribution in place channel conflict could be a major concern, for new distribution strategies the other concern of product support also will play a major part in the development of the strategy. As with all international or product distribution changes, protecting existing partners always complicates the decision making process.

Product suitability

Ensuring that your product is suitable for the target marketplace is the next step in the process. This will include factors specific for e-commerce, but also others that are important to ensure success.

BUSINESS MODEL IMPACT WITH INTERNATIONAL E-COMMERCE

Business model	Impact on direct sales to new international clients	Impact on current international channels	Impact on direct sales to current international clients
New international e-commerce business model	No channel conflict, but complete system from demand through fulfillment has to be developed	Not applicable	Not applicable
Existing direct business model (non web based)	Could create conflict with current distributionsystems in place, if not factored into the design	Not applicable	Could create conflict with current distribution systems in place, if not factored into the design
Existing indirect business model	Could create conflict with current distribution systems in place, if not factored into the design	Needs to be developed considering existing channels and support that is in place	Could create conflict with current distribution systems in place, if not factored into the design

Source: Harvard Computing Group 1999

A moderate amount of research should provide information to determine the most attractive markets. This will also provide you with good input on the scale and cost of what is needed to customize the product or service to enter the market.

FACTORS AFFECTING PRODUCT SUITABILITY IN INTERNATIONAL MARKETPLACE

Pricing	Is product competitive in local marketplace?
Competitiveness	How should product be priced and packaged for local market needs?
Language	Is localization required to enter the market? What will the cost and scope of translation needed for success?
Market size	Is the marketplace large enough to warrant the investment?
Internet infrastructure	Are there a suitable number of Internet users to make the transactions happen (including good connections via ISPs)?
Cultural infrastructure	Is e-commerce accepted as a means of doing business? What is the current rate of e-commerce growth in this market?
Existing distribution systems	Are there current distribution systems in place that will help (or hinder) an e-commerce initiative?
Shipping/fulfillment	How will the product be shipped and delivered to the client?
Support	What local support is required?
Volatility	Is the market volatile? (Either financially or politically)

Source: Harvard Computing Group 1999

Pricing and legal factors

Developing pricing strategies for international distribution via the web is no more complex (or simple) than any other environment. However, if this is the first foray into the international marketplace, then several issues need to be determined.

The first phase will comprise of the basic business issues of:

- single or custom pricing strategy for each market

- margin goals

- cost of sale

- cost of support

- market share goals

Once these have been determined, other pricing factors come into play including:

- competition

- what will the current marketplace stand?

- currency transactions

- import duties

- export duties

- shipping costs

Many companies are concerned that once their US list price is shown on their site, it will be very difficult to obtain a different (i.e. higher) price from other markets. There is no question that once a US list price is shown, then a benchmark has been placed for international prospects to consider. However, there are other issues to consider that cause changes in price and support.

Some examples of these are shown in the table below.

Contracts are another area needing caution to avoid potential problems. The best approach is to keep things simple and understandable. This will reduce confusion and potential problems. Many countries have very different commercial trading practices, and it is important to become famil-

---

EXAMPLES OF VARIABLES AND THE IMPACT ON PRICING STRATEGIES

Variables	Impact on pricing
Warranty	Increased price for international support
One single price based on US list	If the transaction is in dollars, no currency issues arise
Support	Local support has different price
Shipping and handling	Cost will increase based on client requirements (air or sea freight)
Customs and import/ export duties	Usually paid by the consumer or importer

Source: Harvard Computing Group 1999

---

iar with them before presenting them with an unsatisfactory method of purchase or terms and conditions

The legal profession and governments worldwide are trying their best to come to terms with the complex array of problems associated with trading on the web. The web changes many rules of trading that were based on the physical transfer of goods across borders for many years. This is definitely a "watch this space" topic.

Cultural change

In earlier chapters we have discussed extensively the issue of change, and how it affects our focus on the future. One area never to be underestimated is that of the organizational culture. Determining how best to take advantage of change in the operation is known as a soft skill. Despite being known as a soft skill, we often feel like using something harder when trying to convince others to change their behavior.

Developing new systems for e-commerce requires considerable change in many aspects of a business. Smart managers will understand that the resistance or willingness to deal with these changes can have a major impact of how you go about encouraging others to go down the same path.

Smart quotes

Five frogs sat on a log. One decided to jump. How many frogs are left? [The answer is] "Five. There's a difference between deciding to jump and actually jumping. Inspired leaders know how to get total commitment, so that no frogs are left on the corporate log. Zero-frog leadership."

Gay Hendricks, *The Corporate Mystic* (from David Firth, *Smart Things to Know about Change*)

About organization culture

- How ready is the organization to consider change?
- Will change be readily accepted in the operation?
- What will be the easiest way to gain agreement for major change in the operation?

Some operations have very conservative approaches and processes tightly ingrained in their cultures. For example, some regulated industries have not really considered the basic concerns of competition. Now as deregulation begins to occur in many countries, the culture change in these organizations has a direct relationship to their ability to become competitive after deregulation.

E-commerce can cause all these things to change, but organizations need to be prepared for this to happen.

By understanding the culture in the organization, it is easier to determine where the points of success are in the operation.

Roadmap and timeline

Determining the roadmap and timeline for your e-commerce system requires that *business goals, processes and technology be aligned*.

Most e-commerce projects may be divided into seven phases:

1. technology awareness

2. needs assessment/business case preparation

Go to market strategy

Shorthand for a plan of how you will bring your e-commerce solution to potential clients and position it successfully against the competition.

Smart things
to say about
e-commerce

3. functional requirements specification

4. go to market strategy

5. development

6. implementation/training

7. market roll-out.

The timeline shown here is for sample purposes only; however, unlike some more traditional information technology solutions, most e-commerce applications have to be developed quickly and have to respond to market needs. This factor is very material to most operations with their e-commerce strategies, as many want to move fast, if only because they have already spent too much time considering alternatives with traditional timelines. This timeline would represent a large-scale project; many web projects could be completed in a much more collapsed timeframe than the one shown below.

SEVEN STEP CHECK LIST WITH SAMPLE TIMELINE

Technology Awareness	Needs assessment/ business case preparation	Functional requirements specification	Go to market strategy	Development	Implementation, training and testing	Market roll out
Week 1	Weeks 2-4	Weeks 4-8	Weeks 8-12	Weeks 12-20	Weeks 20-22	Weeks 22-24

Smart things
to say about
e-commerce

Avoid:

- lengthy procurement processes that extend the timelines for system decision making processes
- releasing generic RFPs that will cause you to "churn" in the evaluation cycle
- starting development before you know what you want to build.

Technology awareness

As we discussed in Chapter 6, a technology awareness program can bring staff from a wide range of backgrounds and interests and get everyone onto the same playing field quickly. In ideal circumstances the seminar will not only cover the relevant technologies for e-commerce, but also be pertinent to your industry or goals from the system.

Needs assessment/business case preparation

Your business case should include a summary of the recommendations, high-level descriptions of the applications including costs, savings, return on investment, payback period, time to implement, expected outcomes and your hard/soft benefits analysis.

In addition to the needs assessment and business case preparation recommended in Chapter 6, some preliminary review of a go to market strategy should be included at this stage.

Smart
answers to
tough
questions

Q: How can I take months from my decision making and implementation of my e-commerce system?

A: Define a tight game plan, a short time line that does not add extra steps to the process. Ensure that your e-commerce needs are well defined early in the process and tested in the market.

Functional requirements specification

Once the business case is complete, your organization should be armed with the information needed to decide which projects should be tackled. During this phase, functional specifications will be prepared for all, or some of the applications defined in the business case. These specifications can then be distributed to vendors and integrators to receive proposals for hardware, software, development, and/or implementation costs. IT staff may also use the specifications to develop the applications internally.

The functional requirements specifications include more detailed infrastructure recommendations formulated to ensure support of the existing applications and any new or enhanced applications identified in the plan.

Good questions to help develop functional requirements:

- Who uses the application?
- How is the information going to be accessed? Internal at the office, or remotely from the road/home?
- What are their interactivity requirements? How often must the information be updated?
- What are the security requirements for the data? What security is required in the user interface, or at the server? What are the security requirements for data transmitted using the Internet or intranet?
- What information should be captured?
- What are the interface requirements, import and export?
- What hardware is currently in use, what are the upgrade plans?
- What are the bandwidth requirements?
- Can, will, or should databases be replicated to decrease bandwidth requirements?
- Is public access a requirement?
- What are the back-up requirements for the information? Are there applications that require redundancy to ensure there is little or no down time? What are the acceptable down times for each application, if any?

KILLER
QUESTIONS

I believe that creating a good functional specification will reduce cost and ultimately save money in time to market and effective adoption of the technology.

Building prototypes

You should seriously consider the development of prototypes in your e-commerce program. They can help gain agreement on sensitive issues of such as user interface, look and feel, and address the target audience by gaining consensus for the system. Prototypes consist of dummy views and show users how the site will look, be navigated and what content is included.

One great value of the myriad of authoring tools on the market, is that relatively inexperienced individuals can produce sites that "look and feel" like a professional one. These tools allow users to change the way that they look by predefined templates, artwork and typographic treatment. Many will have thematic approaches for different industries and audiences. These tools can be used to help you with the development of your prototypes, without tremendous investment in the production system tools that you are likely to use for interactive and complex e-commerce applications.

Smart things
to say about
e-commerce

Why prototypes make sense:

- they ensure that the working group agrees on direction
- they provide a visual aid to show how and where things will be
- they yield great feedback for the webmaster in the development process
- they allow change to occur quickly when necessary.

Example of prototype for new business to business e-commerce site

Go to market strategy (GTM)

You should consider the go to market strategy as early as possible in the process, ideally as part of the development of your business case. A go to market strategy provides the vehicle for process change, marketing, sales programs and other aspects of the introduction to be successful. Do not leave this to the last minute. You will regret it if you do. When you integrate a GTM strategy into the rest of your plan, time frames can be collapsed and the risks of not meeting expectations are reduced dramatically.

SMART VOICES

Include these items in your go to market strategy:

- marketing plan and tactical actions
- press plan and tour
- introduction to existing and new clients
- pricing and packaging information
- site traffic promotion
- introductory offers (if appropriate)
- partner programs (if appropriate)
- internal promotion and explanation of the new site and purpose
- validation of the business model.

A smart thing to do is a continuous test of the validity of your business offering. If we only had to worry about the technology changing in the Internet space, life would be relatively easy. The reality is the business offerings of the Internet are also changing rapidly. Since the spring of 1999, when this book was first started, these two examples show how much is changing and how fast it is changing.

- *Intranet offerings*

  These were offered as licensed products in the spring, now are being offered as hosted products with a zero entry cost.

- *Extranet collaboration products*

  These were offered (and are still offered as licensed software products), but are now also available free as a hosted product.

Most firms are now employing almost real-time target marketing techniques to ensure that their GTM strategy will still be relevant by the time that the product is available. *Willingness to change from your original plan is important.*

Development

Once the specifications are firm, and the green light is given, development can start. As discussed earlier, the skills and cost to maintain the site may have a profound impact on the approach you take. Many companies have spent significant dollars on the development of their first e-commerce system only to find that it did not meet the market needs. Guess what – they then had to build it all over again. The cost of learning in this business should not be underestimated. However, hiring the best and most appropriate development resources (if you are not doing it in-house) will reduce the risk and likely turn out to be money well spent.

Smart quotes

Any company I've started has deviated from its mission. The key to success is being able to deviate.

Jim Clark

Different companies and individuals have various approaches for the building systems. Today, all but the most complex systems are built in relatively short timeframes.

Implementation and training

Once the development is over, the implementation, training and roll-out of the system has to be managed. You should consider adding a beta best phase to your program to ensure that good acceptance of the system will occur. This will also allow for further feedback on the characteristics of the e-commerce system, so that you can "fine-tune" the final application before going live.

If the usability of and navigation aspects of the system have been well designed, there is often no need for user-based training of the product or

Smart things
to say about
e-commerce

Testing e-commerce systems:

- purchase procedures
- access controls
- navigation and critical links
- affinity and related sites
- all security aspects of the system
- pricing
- configuration management (if applicable)
- legal agreements and contracts
- confidentiality and privacy concerns.

application. However, there are many business to business systems that are considerably more complex than those of the business to consumer application on the market that require user training.

Market Roll-out

Once the application has been tested effectively, you are now ready to release the system to the world. Launching a site can be an exciting and a trying time for all concerned. Do not assume that e-commerce systems are "done" when you reach this phase, this is just the beginning. Change in the e-commerce world is the norm, being ready and able to change according to market and company needs ultimately define long-term success.

The whole topic of e-commerce is a complex one, and a wild ride. We have not been faced with such a changing landscape of technology, business rules and work process in our lifetimes. The chameleon nature of the environment will ultimately cause us to engage. Perhaps the definition of e-business and e-commerce will drop the "e-" eventually. Because this is such a new way of doing business, we consider it very differently from other forms of commerce. Over time this will change, and the Internet and the WWW become the norm and not the exception to our business strategies. Until then we will continue to learn, adapt and execute in Internet cycle times.

8
Out There

I never planned to write this chapter, but my publishers thought that it would be fun. Two things concerned me about this project. One was to try and write something that would still be relevant more than three months after it was published, a significant problem with the Internet, technology and business changing so rapidly. The other worry was writing something that was predictive to extending the relevance of the book. So, please treat anything from here on out as part science, part fiction, perhaps science fiction.

Looking to the future of the Internet reminds me of time-lapse photographic experiments conducted at college, the flowers blooming, a season passing, a storm brewing. The analogy for the Internet could be the same time-lapse program, but instead continents forming and oceans rising and falling.

I use the geographic comparison because that is how it is. We are building new continents that did not exist before. These continents have communities that are evolving and devolving, growing and changing. The Internet will evolve based on several variables that we know that we have to deal with today. These include:

- technology

- work processes

- government policies and programs.

Technology

The technology components of the Internet continue to create tremendous interest and excitement. There is no question that the Internet and supporting technology have allowed enormous networks of users to be linked together in a very efficient and scalable manner. The latest systems have all but supplanted earlier designs based on client/server architectures replacing them with n-tier systems that form the basis of most large-scale systems.

While database technologies have become more robust, little has been done to advance the use of object oriented databases. These databases have some great capabilities to inherit ways to manipulate and intelligently re-

Smart things to say about e-commerce

About the future:

Most systems will be developed using n-tier architectures in the coming 2–3 years. These will integrate browser desktop, application logic and distributed database systems.

use information. Sometime soon, extensive use of object-oriented databases will take off on the web. When this happens, the ability not just to deliver and transfer information will start to occur, but the context of how to use it as it arrives with the information. This will be a truly remarkable step in the development and manipulation of web content.

Content repositories

The demand for content and requirements to manage it effectively will create new breeds of content servers and syndication systems. These systems will allow companies to find and quickly license content and deliver it directly to the sites that need it. The technology to accomplish this already exists in the most advanced servers on the market. Today most of these servers are dedicated to supply chain or complex applications in information publishing.

Ad servers

Next generation Ad servers will provide a wide range of capabilities that will further customize the delivery of information to the target audience. This will include tight links between personalized databases and the ad server technology, allowing customized advertising and content to be delivered to the audience.

Video conferencing and distance learning

With the availability of greater bandwidth for Internet users , today's limitations surrounding on-demand video conferencing and distance learning will change. Even the smallest businesses will be able to afford video conferencing and other distance conferencing tools to good effect. As quality digital cameras become affordable, most organizations will be able to use this technology on a daily basis.

Distance learning will become a normal method of delivering courses and information to remote workers and others who do not have the time to travel to meeting and educational locations. Improved interaction with students using chat, video and feedback mechanisms will improve the retention problems associated with these technologies in the past.

Free shared services

The pricing of Internet systems and services will continue to shift. In the past 24 months, we have seen free email, calendaring, groupware and now intranets. As Internet based companies look for ways to reduce their cost of sale and entry points in the marketplace, more software and services will be offered free, or on usage basis. This way we will pay only for the software and services that we use, an alternative to the current licensing schemes that require the deployment of complex systems before users can gain access.

Hosting services (timesharing is back!)

Unless you have been in the computer industry for 20 years or more, timesharing may not be a familiar concept. Timesharing services provided shared use of a computer system and charged the customer based on their use of those resources. As computers became more affordable and more firms brought their computing functions in-house, the services declined. However, timesharing is on its way back, only this time bigger and better. The Internet hosts the biggest timesharing applications in the world today, and more are coming down the road. Two factors are causing the rapid adoption of more applications to be hosted outside the organization. The first is the reduced cost of providing high performance network access to a site that is different from the location of the server, and the second is the very significant support costs associated with adding new Internet software products and services.

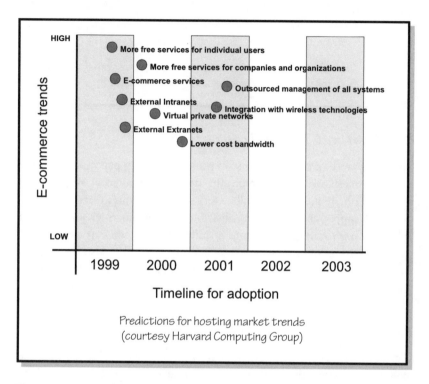

HIGH

E-commerce trends

- More free services for individual users
- More free services for companies and organizations
- E-commerce services
- Outsourced management of all systems
- External Intranets
- Integration with wireless technologies
- Virtual private networks
- External Extranets
- Lower cost bandwidth

LOW

1999 2000 2001 2002 2003

Timeline for adoption

Predictions for hosting market trends
(courtesy Harvard Computing Group)

Tomorrow's timesharing market will consist of an expanded version of the hosting market. (This is currently being defined as the Application Service Provider segment.) Hosting firms will offer more services to meet the ever-increasing requirements of their clients. As bandwidth becomes more affordable, it will encourage the remote use of systems that have traditionally been located internally. Applications such as intranets will be offered to small and large companies alike. The additional replication, mirroring and load-balancing capabilities of these services will allow for clients to start small, but have the option of scaling systems as their needs grow.

DSL

Digital subscriber line: a high-performance Internet connection provided over current telephone circuits and lines at a very affordable price.

Instant extranets and collaboration tools

Extranets were once difficult and expensive to set up particularly for the small business owners who typically often have limited IT resources to manage them. In the future, it will be very simple for firms to set up extranets for their supply chain partners, distributors, customers or joint project partners. Improved technology to install and deploy an extranet will encourage setting up of semi-permanent secure networks. Also hosting services and software firms will offer products that allow their clients to specify users of the extranet and their access controls.

Lower cost bandwidth

The cost of access to the Internet is currently low is most countries, but the connection speeds still cause envy between the regular dial-up user and the corporate user on the network. Well, not for much longer. The availability of new technologies such as DSL and broadband (cable modems) will change the entry cost for high performance bandwidth. Existing technologies such as ISDN and frame-relay will have to adjust their price points to remain competitive in this expanding marketplace.

The concept of each organization having affordable, high-speed access to the Internet will be with us in the next 2 years, at least in the North American marketplace. Billions of dollars are currently being spent on infrastructure, which will translate to a very competitive marketplace for data services and bandwidth. It will also make applications such as video-

PDA

Personal digital assistant: a hand-held computing device to provide convenient computing resources without the need for a laptop or larger computer.

Smart things
to say about
e-commerce

conferencing and multi-media apps like distance learning more popular as the barrier to entry drops, expanding the user base quickly.

Wireless and hand-held systems

The recent explosion in hand-held PDAs and wireless systems continues to show no signs of abating. As operating systems become more powerful and intelligent devices incorporate improved computers, this trend will continue.

Wireless technology is now used for many differing Internet applications, but will gain more ground as the digital wireless networks become more reliable and available around the world. The world has moved on from the pager to the cellular telephone. Advanced versions of these devices will include personal contact management, a telephone, pager, email reader and interfaces to peripherals such as printers for the traveler. Today these are expensive options: in the future they will be very affordable.

XML

The eXtensible Markup Language is the frontrunner of how systems will be built in the future. Most of the limitations of HTML have been overcome since in the introduction of this language. More vendors and developers will use it to good effect in the future. For the long term maintenance and re-purposing of information, XML does the heavy lifting without the computing gymnastics and performance overhead of earlier systems. It will also bring documents closer to the web publishing business, with great improvements in information interchange. If you have a choice, build your new systems using XML as the foundation. It provides much flexibility and allows you to extend the system easily in the future.

Work processes

Workgroup collaboration

Collaboration will be the name of the game for work processes in the future. As the need to become physically located right next to the work area becomes less important because of the Internet, the need for collaboration increases. Most of us have not been prepared for this transition, it has just happened to us. Unlike our children who have grown up with chat and instant messaging, the workforce is still adjusting to the breakdown in order and structure that the Internet and the collaborative technology brings.

George Carlin (the comedian) once quipped "Men are from earth, women are from earth: Deal with it." That just sums up the situation with the Internet and collaboration; we cannot ignore it, we have to deal with it.

The new work processes and work patterns that Internet based technology gives us is mind-blowing: shopping, research, finding a life partner,

Smart quotes

The newest innovations, which we label information technologies, have begun to alter the manner in which we do business and create value, often in ways not readily foreseeable even five years ago.

Alan Greenspan (Chairman, Federal Reserve Board, May 6, 1999)

buying a car and maintaining an airplane. We are in a connected workspace and can work with almost anyone we want. We have become familiar with this concept for electronic mail, but we have not made the transition for these work patterns. Knowledge management, research, project management and publishing will be a few of the applications that are impacted by these new work processes. The technology will not be the limiting factor, just the behavioral changes and the way that we want to use it.

Fortunes will to be won or lost based on our ability to make these changes in the workplace. There is a reason that change management has become one of the hottest practice areas among consultants, many organizations want to change quickly and do not know how. Learning to change and exploit the tools will become a great challenge for the workplace in the next five years.

Buying patterns

A consolidation of buying patterns is likely to occur because of the Internet. With large numbers of consumers already doing their shopping "homework" on the Internet, the ability to influence their decisions will increase.

Time is one of the major reasons why organizations acquire new technology and deploy it in the workplace. Time saved is one of the greatest benefits to most organizations. In using the Internet to buy services and goods, many companies are not just saving money by reducing the actual cost of processing the order (in some examples, this can be higher than the value of the goods). They are also enforcing purchasing policies to the buyer in the organization. Companies from office supply stores to computer vendors they all want to bring their "store" into your organization. They will make it easy to allow the company to set up an account and provide these decisions on-line. Buying patterns will continue to change for many reasons including: convenience, timeliness, accuracy, price and service.

Supply chain of the week

The Internet is creating new work process opportunities to build new networks of partners and suppliers in a very short period. For many businesses, selection of partners and how you work with them takes several months and lots of due diligence to make a decision. However, with the Internet and a flexible range of services, many companies can repackage their service and product offerings to add them to others and make new products or services.

Government policies and programs

Many governments are trying hard to provide policies that will make it easy for companies to operate their Internet businesses from their localities. Much of the concerns today are tied to taxation policies on the Internet. The United States currently is still under a moratorium for Internet taxes, which expires in 2001. Debates continue to determine what might happen if the government decided to tax e-commerce on the Internet. Business-to-business e-commerce would not be affected, as there is no corporate taxation in the US for business-to-business commerce.

The issues of privacy, intellectual property and piracy continue to be engaged by the US and other governments. The privacy issues in particular can cause some consternation for companies profiling and marketing their clients demographics to others.

Policies and their interpretation run the gamut from protecting the right to free speech to protecting the rights of the individual. The Internet and related technologies will continue to push the boundaries of these issues, dependent on individuals and organizations' needs and expectations.

It may happen

Let us consider how a typical day in the Internet future could unfold.

Monday morning on April 9, 2001 to my day starts out:

1. 7.00 a.m. I awake to my net appliance starting my TV with relevant programming, a small dose of national news, updates on the four countries we are working with currently, and a broadcast reminder of major events today, overlaid on my monitor.

2. The program for breakfast has started up the rest of the network in the house. The coffee maker is now running, breakfast items are removed from the fridge in convenient packages delivered by the Internet food service. These are dated and sorted according to the diet my wife put me on last year.

3. My first appointment at the office at 9.00 a.m. flashes on the TV screen. I head for the shower: as I open the shower door, the net radio/phone kicks in broadcasting other key appointments in my calendar for the week.

4. Heading to work now in the car. The netphone rings again. My 9.00 a.m. appointment is running late with traffic problems in Boston. As she is on the netphone, I put her on hold, send a routing agent to Mapquest to redirect her, based on the traffic patterns for the morning. This sends directions in real time to her net travel computer. The directions agent stays with her computer for the duration of the journey, ensuring she avoids new bottlenecks. She is relieved, and less frustrated as she gets off the freeway and uses the back roads to reach us almost on time.

5. 11.30 a.m. Netconference with Seattle: interactive video, voice and data conference regarding a new project with a client. The large screen monitor makes the 45-minute meeting very effective. We all agree that we did not need the 6-hour flight to meet and set up an extranet on the spot and a virtual private network for the joint project we have agreed.

6. 2.00 p.m. Sales review meeting. We sent the sales agents out on the net again last week and now we are reviewing the potential projects that have been submitted. Based on our best fit and the resources available, we provide multi-media responses and references to the prospective clients.

7. 3.00 p.m. Received a request to provide a speaker in Ireland for an upcoming conference. Place an agent request to our resource planning system, provides best-fit consultants and availability. The support and travel costs have been estimated electronically to provide the information back in real-time to the group in Ireland.

8. 6.00 p.m. Head out of the office again, this time for my son's soccer practice. As we drive in the car, he listens to his programmed Internet radio, and I get a voice update on tomorrow's activities.

9. 6.15 p.m. We leave the car for soccer practice. The coach orders all parents to leave their net devices in their vehicles and enjoy the practice session.

Although this day may sound somewhat like science fiction, we already have web radio, web TV, grocery delivery services, integrated cell phones and wireless services, and increasingly sophisticated tracking systems in our cars. Check and see how much of this is affordable and in place within two years, after all it's really 14 web years away. A lot could happen in that time.

Where to focus

Making decisions where to make your next move in the e-commerce space is not a trivial process. No doubt, it will be easier for you if you already have an established organization, particularly one with some brand recognition. It is much easier to establish an effective presence if you have somewhere to start.

I trust that this book has provided you some guidelines of where to begin an e-commerce program, and how some of these ingredients influence each other. Understanding these interdependent factors is an essential element of a successful strategy. Unlike almost any other applications, e-commerce requires a very well cooked blend of people, processes and technology: one that your target users, be they business partners or consumers, need to accept and embrace.

Our imaginations are without doubt one of the most important elements in the next generation of e-commerce systems. In many cases, the very framework of our existing environments limits us, and thus causes us to consider only solutions that will "fit it". Building successful e-commerce systems is neither an art nor a science. They are a blend of people, processes and technology. Enjoy your time working with the blender.

Recommended Reading

Cliff Allen, Deborah Kania and Beth Yaeckel, *Internet World Guide to One-to-One Web Marketing*, John Wiley 1998, ISBN 0-471-25166-6.

John Hagel and Marc Singer, *Net Worth*, Harvard Business School Press.

Christina Ford Haylock and Len Muscarella, *NetSuccess*, Adams Media Corporation

Ravi Kalakota and Andrew B. Whinston, *Electronic Commerce: A Manager's Guide*, Addison Wesley 1997, ISBN 0-201-88067-9.

David R. Kosiur, *Understanding Electronic Commerce* (Strategic Technology Series), Microsoft Press 1997, ISBN 1572315607.

Daniel C. Lynch and Leslie Lundquist, *Digital Money: The New Era of Internet Commerce*, John Wiley 1996, ISBN 0-471-14178-X.

Christopher Meyer and Stan Davis, *Blur: The Speed of Change in the Connected Economy*, Capstone.

William Miller, *Flash of Brilliance*, Perseus Books.

Geoffery Moore, *Inside the Tornado*, Harper Business.

Don Peppers, and Martha Rogers, *Enterprise One to One: Tools for Competing in the Interactive Age*, Currency Books 1997, ISBN 0-385-48205-1.

Frederick F. Reichheld, *The Loyalty Effect: The Hidden Force Behind Growth, Profits, and Lasting Value*, Harvard Business School Press 1996, ISBN 0875844480.

Peter M. Senge, *The Fifth Discipline*, DoubleDay.

Patricia B. Seybold, *Customers.com: How to Create a Profitable Business Strategy for the Internet and Beyond*, Random House 1998, ISBN 0-8129-3037-1.

Thomas M. Siebel, *Cyber Rules: Strategies for Excelling at E-Business*, Doubleday.

Glossary

Access provider – a company that provides connectivity to the Internet. Customers of access providers pay a fee and are then granted access to the Internet through an electronic account defined and managed by the providers.

Active-X – multi-media extensions for web browsers provided by Microsoft Corporation to improve web site browsing experience.

Asymmetric digital subscriber line (ADSL) – provides high-bandwidth connections to the Internet, but uses twisted copper wiring so that they can use regular phone lines. Bellcore Labs in New Jersey initially developed this cost-effective method of bringing bandwidth to homes and small businesses in 1993.

Andreessen, Marc – led the team that created Netscape Navigator through his company, Mosaic Communications Corporation. Before creating

Netscape Navigator, Andreessen created NCSA Mosaic at the National Center for Supercomputing applications.

ARPANET (Advanced Research Projects Agency Network) – the first Internet, developed in the 1960s as a way for US authorities to communicate with each other in the aftermath of a nuclear attack. This formed the basis that has subsequently evolved into today's Internet.

Authentication – the name of the process to verify the identity of a user as they log onto a network.

Bandwidth – describes the amount of data that can travel through the Internet or communications network in a specified period of time. This is usually measured in seconds.

Berners-Lee, Tim – while working in Geneva, Switzerland at CERN, the European Particle Physics Laboratory, Berners-Lee created the World Wide Web.

Bookmarks – provide the user with the ability to mark their favorite pages and web sites so that they may be accessed quickly and easily. Most browsers support the bookmark function.

Brick and mortar – a term used to describe traditional stores and methods of selling and distributing products. Barnes and Noble who sell books through their stores as well as on-line can be described as using both brick and mortar and e-commerce strategies in their business.

Brochureware – the act of putting your corporate literature in basic static form directly to a web site. Often bores visitors to death, and causes rapid exits from the site.

Browser – a software application, (such as Netscape Communicator and Microsoft Internet Explorer which interprets the HTML and web documents so that they may operate on a point and click interface). A browser can be used to run complete software applications with extensions and plug-ins.

Bulletin board system – often referred to as a BBS, this system allows others to read, comment and electronically post new messages to the group reading them. Often used for interest groups, customer support or professional groups, BBS systems represent a low cost and effective collaboration forum for the Internet.

Business to business – the portion of the Internet market that effects transactions between business operations and their partners in marketing, sales, development, manufacturing and support. The largest portion of the Internet marketplace, and the fastest growing.

Channels – Can have two meanings in the Internet world.

A *channel* is a web site designed to deliver content from the Internet to your computer, similar to subscribing to a favorite Web site. Typically, it is not necessary to subscribe the web, but by connecting to the "channel" suggested, content can be delivered to your desktop browser.

Channels of distribution: a distribution channel is a method of providing your product or service to the target user of the system. This could be an on-line mall, portal, your own brand site or distribution supply chain.

Chat – chat systems are used to allow users of networks and the Internet to communicate in real time. Messages today are typically posted via a desktop window with other members of the group. The message will then appear in the open chat windows of others in that particular group for review and further comment.

Click-thru – the act of clicking (with a mouse) on a particular graphic or element on a web-page. These are measured to determine the effectiveness of advertising, content and traffic patterns of individual web sites.

Communicator – Netscape's browser, collaboration, and communication software developed in January 1997.

Community – electronic forum where individuals and groups gather to find relevant and pertinent information. They are often segmented by interest or geography.

Content – the actual material, text, graphics and other multi-media that make up a web site.

Content management – the system and method by which content is updated, changed and re-posted to the web site.

Cookie – stores personal preferences for Internet information and communication tools in files in a browser's folder. A text file that contains the information of user's preferences is created and is stored in memory while the browser is running. In addition to personal preferences, cookies can also save information such as the date that the web site was visited, what purchases were made, what ad banners were clicked on, what files were downloaded, and the information viewed.

CPM – cost per thousand impressions. A measurement of how many times someone has viewed your banner ad via a browser.

Cyberspace – coined by William Gibson in 1984, this term is used to describe the place where people interact, communicate, and exchange information using the Internet.

Dial-up networking – allows a PC to dial into its server and connect to the Internet using either SLIP (serial line interface protocol) or PPP (point-to-point protocol) connections. The connection makes it possible for the user to work with any software that supports the communication protocol TCP/IP.

Domain – groups that hosts and local area networks are placed in. All of the computer users of a commercial Internet provider make up a domain.

Domain name – unique name that is used to identify a web site. It contains two or more parts separated by a dot. The existing domain names fit into one of seven categories: educational institutions; commercial organizations; military; government; non-profit organizations; networking organizations; and international organizations. e.g. www.capstone.co.uk.

Early adopters – groups of users and individual that will typically adopt technology and new work processes early in their introduction to the marketplace.

EDI – electronic data interchange – the controlled transfer of data between businesses and organizations via established security standards.

E-business – term now used broadly for the act of doing business using the Internet and other electronic means to conduct business.

Email – electronic mail is the Internet service most widely used. By sending an email, a file is created that will be transmitted and delivered to the electronic mailbox of the person you address. Can also be used to transfer files containing other information such as documents, programs and multi-media data.

E-tailing – Online sales of retail style goods. Many consumer and specialist goods are now available via these on-line e-tailers.

Excite – a popular search engine and portal, which uses keywords to create summaries of each of the web pages and usenet newsgroups the search criteria matches. Excite is one of the most widely used search engines that provides a full range of services, including a comprehensive subject directory.

Extranets – private wide area networks that run on public protocols with the goal of fostering collaboration and information sharing between organizations. A feature of extranets is that companies can allow certain guests to have access to internal data on a controlled basis.

E-zine – online publications in the form of newsletters or magazines that facilitate a new way for communication and interaction to occur on the Internet. e.g. www.salon.com.

FAQ (frequently asked questions) – helpful way for new users to look at questions that are regularly asked, usually saved on a bulletin board or as archived files.

File server – a computer that stores and makes available programs and data available to other computers on a connected network.

Finger – locator used to find people on the Internet. Its most common use is to detect data about a particular user, such as telephone number, whether they are currently logged on or their email address. The individual being "fingered" must have his or her profile on the mail system, otherwise there may be no results to a finger query.

Fire Wall – a software/hardware combination that separates an internal local area network from the external Internet. This is done for security purposes in order to protect a company's network from the outside world, and unauthorized electronic visitors.

FTP (file transfer protocol) – a protocol used on the Internet to transfer many different types of information in the form of files and data. These files and data may contain software, text documents, sound, or images. Used as a way of transferring data from one site to another, this protocol is now transparent to many users using browser-based applications.

Gateway – a hardware or software component that links two otherwise incompatible applications or networks.

Gopher – navigational tool that finds resources and information on the Internet by using a multi-level menu system. The main menu is a list of hyperlinks, each with an icon that describes the type of resource to which the resource connects. The resources that a hyperlink could be connected to might be a text file, a movie or binary file, an image, or an index.

History of the Internet – the Internet was created in the 1960s by the US Department of Defense as a method of sustaining electronic communication after a nuclear attack. The Rand Corporation, the foremost military think tank, created the first communication network that has evolved into today's Internet. After ARPANET, the network that connected four US campuses, was a huge success, research continued into the 1970s. Many large organizations and companies created private computer networks. In the 1980s, ARPANET evolved into the Internet due to the

TCP/IP protocol. The popularity of personal computers and the increasingly powerful network servers made it possible for companies to connect to the Internet. The Internet has grown in popularity at an incredible pace: Microsoft and Netscape have created browsers with increasingly complicated and sophisticated software, making the Internet more accessible.

Home page – using HTML (hypertext markup language), Internet developers are able to create a home page, which is the first page that a user sees after entering a URL for a Web site. (It is now sometimes called the Index page.)

HTML (hypertext markup language) – the language used to create a web page. It is used to format the text of a document, specify links to other documents and describe the structure of the Web page. In addition to these main uses, HTML may also be used to display different types of media, such as images, video and sound.

HTTP (hypertext transfer protocol) – protocol used to transfer information within the world wide web.

Hyperlink – electronic link that can be programmed so that it is possible to make a jump from one document or web page to another. These are primary tools for navigating the Internet.

Impressions – The number of times that an element of a page has been viewed by an individual browser. Often used to count Internet ad placements.

Intranet – Internet based computing networks that are private and secure. Typically used by corporations, government and other organizations, these are based upon Internet standards and provide the means for an organization to make resources more readily available to its employees online.

IP (Internet protocol) – software that divides information into packets. It then transmits this information in its divided form. This is required for all computers on the Internet to communicate.

IP address – an address that identifies each computer on the Internet using a string of four sets of numbers separated by periods.

IRC – acronym for Internet relay chat. Allows individuals to "chat" on the Internet. See *Chat*.

ISP – Internet service providers deliver a wide range of services to individual users and organizations for the Internet. These include web hosting, electronic mail, FTP, and many other e-commerce services.

ISDN (integrated services digital network) – telephone service that has become a popular cost effective solution to traditional dial-up speeds over the Internet. ISDN allows ordinary telephone lines to transmit digital instead of analog signals, thereby permitting much faster dial up and transmission speeds.

Internic – governing body controlling the issue and control of Internet domains and addresses. Currently a partnership between the US government and Network Solutions, Inc.

IT – information technology.

Java – programming language that was created in 1995. Developed by Sun Microsystems, Java is an object-oriented programming language that allows content and software to be distributed through the Internet.

Applications that are written in Java must be run by a Java enabled web browser.

Kermit – a file transfer program that is popular on mainframe computers.

Killer App (application) – incredibly useful, creative program that provides a breakthrough for its users. The first killer app of the Internet was email.

LAN (local area network) – computer network that operates and is located in one specific location. Many of these may be connected together in order to enable users to share resources and information on their network.

Legacy Systems – generally described as an existing computer system that is providing a function for some part of the business. Often, these systems are considered older in nature, but often provide some strategic function to the business. Examples include:

- inventory management systems

- manufacturing resource planning systems (MRP)

- enterprise resource planning (ERP)

- sales automation systems

- help desk systems.

Listserv Mailing Lists – system that distributes email. It manages interactive mailing lists and can either be managed by staff or by a computer program. They are used when dealing with groups that share common interests and want to share information or resources.

MIME –multipurpose Internet mail extension, a standard method to identify the type of data contained in a file based on its extension. MIME is an Internet protocol that allows you to send binary files across the Internet as attachments to Email messages. These files include graphics, programs, sound and video files, as well as electronic office files. MIME allows different types of systems to interpret these different files types successfully.

Mirroring – exact copying of the content of one computer disk to another. Used to back up information in mission-critical systems, and permit the maintenance of others while the system is still running.

Moore's Law – Gordon E. Moore, co-founder of Intel, said in 1965 that he predicted that the processing power of integrated circuits would double every 18 months for the next 10 years. This law has proven true for almost 30 years and is now used in many performance forecasts. Moore's second law is that the cost of production would double every generation.

Multimedia – term used to describe many different forms of media being used for particular applications. Multi-media applications often include graphics, animation, sound and video elements.

Navigator – term used to refer to Netscape Navigator, the browser created by Netscape Communications Corporation (formerly known as Mosaic Communications Corporation), first released in October of 1994.

Newsgroup – electronic discussion group comprising collections of postings to particular topics. These topics are posted to the designated news server for this group. Newsgroups can be an invaluable source of information and advice when trying to resolve problems and get advice.

Newsreader – software program that lets you subscribe to newsgroups, in addition to reading and posting messages to them. Will keep track of groups visited and favorites for simplified navigation when returning and tracking activities in different groups.

Net – abbreviation of Internet.

Netiquette – set of rules users are encouraged to follow if participating in an electronic discussion group or sending email on the Internet.

NIH – not invented here

Node – an individually addressable point on a network. Could be a computer, printer or server on the network.

One-to-one marketing – customization and personalization of both product and prospect requirements to meet an individual set of established needs. Once matched, a one-to-one marketing program delivers an exact marketing message, with the appropriate product to meet the prospect's needs.

Packet – term used to describe data being transferred over a network in a unit.

Packet switching – a communications paradigm used to minimize latency and optimize the use of bandwidth available in a network. It does this by individually routing a packet between hosts using the most expedient route. Once the packets are sent, the destination computer reassembles the packets into their appropriate sequence.

Password – a word or code that is secret used to log on to a network. The system checks the word and, if approved, the user has access to the network.

PDAs – personal digital assistants are used to provide relevant computer functions to the individual without the overhead of a laptop or local computer. These now include email, contact information, paging, web browsing and access to remote corporate applications.

Personalization – customization of web information to specifically meet the needs and desires of the individual user.

Plug-Ins – by extending the standard capabilities of a web browser, the plug-in permits the running of other programs and many multi-media applications through the web browsers.

POP (point of presence) – the location of the Internet server.

Portal – major visiting center for Internet users. The very large portals started life as search engines, AltaVista, AOL, CompuServe, Excite, Infoseek, Lycos, Magellan, and Yahoo are examples of major portals.

PPP (point-to-point protocol) – Internet communication protocol for transferring network data over serial point-to-point links.

Pull technology – describes the type of technology used in the Internet, where users are searching for and requesting information to be downloaded to their computer.

Push technology – delivery of information to potential consumers via electronic means. Often involves the automated transmission of new data on particular topic on a regular basis, or some pre-determined event.

Quality of service – defines the level of service for an individual, voice, data or video connection when using a telecommunications supplier.

Realvideo – technology that allows users to see video as it is being downloaded.

Replication – describes the process of controlled copying of certain elements of a web site, database or other collection of information. A technique that can provide portions of a system to be automatically distributed to the area that needs it for performance or other reasons.

ROM (read only memory) – a memory chip that stores data concerning instructions and data included at the time of manufacturing that cannot be easily be changed.

Robot – a program that is designed to automatically go out and explore the Internet for a specific purpose. Some robots that record and index all of the contents of the network to create a searchable database, these robots are called spiders.

Router – a system at the intersection of two networks that works to determine which path is most efficient for data when traveling to its destination.

Search directories – subject indexes on the web that allow users to search for information by entering a keyword into a query box on their site. The directory searches through keyword matches in their database only.

Search engines – search world wide web site, usenet newsgroups, and other Internet resources to match descriptor words. Many also rank the matches in likely order of relevance, making it easier for the user to know what sites are likely to be most helpful.

Server – a program that functions in a client-server information exchange model whose function is to provide information and execute functions for computer attached to the network.

Shareware – software that is made available, by the developers, to users at no cost. Manufacturers of shareware often ask users to review the applications and sometimes request a fee of $10–$25. Shareware is available on web sites, such as www.jumbo.com, www.shareware.com, and www.tucows.com.

SMTP (simple mail transport protocol) – the protocol for Internet email, where the host name of the Internet provider's mail server must be designated in order to send mail.

Spam – the practice of sending email or posting messages for purely commercial gain, often to very large groups of uninterested users.

Spider – programs designed to browse the Internet and look for information to add to a search tool's database.

Spoofing – slang for someone impersonating another on the Internet. Typically used in electronic mail applications.

Streaming – where a plug-in is used to watch a video in real time as it is downloaded, instead of having to store it as a file.

Stickiness – general term to describe the characteristics of a web site to attract and keep users in the area. Also a measurement of how many users return to the site for more information or products.

Synchronous communication – simultaneous communication using applications such as Internet Relay Chat, net phone and video conferencing where communication occurs at the same time.

Subscribe – term used to describe the act of requesting a subscription to a listserv mailing list.

Targeted marketing – development of marketing programs by identifying segments in specific markets and designing the product or service to specifically meet these needs.

Templates – pre-defined application components that allow rapid development and deployment of computer based systems.

T1 line – a high-speed digital connection that can transmit data at a rate of 1.5 million bps (bits per second). Often used by small and medium size organizations, very fast file transfers can be made using this type of connection.

T3 line – a very high-speed connection capable of transmitting data at a rate of 45 million bits per second. Good enough to transmit real time video, this type of connection is usually reserved for large organizations.

TCP/IP (transmission control protocol/ Internet protocol) – set of protocols that allow computers of any make or model to communicate with each other over the Internet. TCP packages the data to be sent and IP provides the addressing information about where the packages are to be sent.

Telnet – allows users to log onto different computers and run resident programs. Although this is not as lauded as the world wide web and requires commands to navigate, it is essential for Internet travel.

Tunneling – a secure mechanism to allow transmission of data across points of access on the Internet.

URLs (uniform resource locators) – the standard form for addresses on the Internet that provide the addressing system for other Internet protocols.

Virus – a program created to cause problems on the computer systems they invade. Virus protection has become a major component in maintaining the health of computer systems everywhere.

Veronica (very easy rodent oriented netwide index to computerized archives) – a network utility that lets individuals search all of more than 6,000 gopher servers in the world.

Virtual private networks – private networks that allow users to purchase bandwidth and access, often through their Internet connection, without the need to purchase dedicated network cabling or systems.

VRML (virtual reality modeling language) – language that allows users to experience a simulated three-dimensional environment on the computer. This was first developed for video games and now has advanced, creating a non-profit VRML consortium with more than 50 companies.

WAIS (wide area information servers) – a network information retrieval that allows searching for keywords or phrases. These are indexed in special files. Unlike gopher, WAIS searches the full text of files that it indexes, thereby providing a much larger group of documents for the user to select. This method is the most popular method used by large search engines on the web.

Wallets – enable shoppers on the Internet to automatically debit their accounts using e-money. The wallet contains electronic money which is usually deposited in advance, and is replenished as the account needs it. This is likely to become a more common form of shopping in the future.

WAN (wide area network) – comprising local networks that are connected to other local networks by high-speed telephone lines.

Web server – a server that is connected to the Internet. It contains world wide web documents.

Whiteboard – electronic equivalent to a chalkboard, whiteboards provide visual communication and interaction over networks.

Wired – term used to describe users who are attached to their computers or use the computer and the web as in integral part of their lifestyle.

World wide web – a collection of protocols and standards that make it possible to view and retrieve information from the Internet. By being linked together in a hypermedia system, this information can be used through the world wide web.

WYSIWYG (what you see is what you get) – term used to refer to text and graphics that will print in the same format as it is seen on the screen.

XML (extensible markup language) – describes the format and presentation, and provides application control over the content of the documents and systems using this language. Much more powerful than HTML, XML is likely to be the next generation language for the web and business applications.

Index

goals 37–40, 44–5, 139–41
governments, trends 50, 200–201
Greenspan, Alan 198
Gretzky, Wayne 33
groupware 16, 18–19, 66
growth, Internet 6–7, 32–3, 99, 192–8
GTM *see* go to market strategy

hard benefits, business case 144–54
Harvard Computing Group xvii
healthcare industry 49
help desks 66, 162–3, 171
Hendricks, Gay 179
history, Internet 1–19, 71–3
Hoffer, Eric x
Hogan, Paul xv
horizontal applications, concept 22
Horowitz, Ed 81
hosting services 63, 105–6, 194–5
    concept 13–14
    costs 35
HotBot 72
HTML *see* hypertext markup language
human resources
    cultural issues 45–51, 132–5
    future prospects 198–200
    internal/external alternatives 156–7
    intranets 124–5
    IT staff 121
    strategy 132–6, 148
hypertext markup language (HTML) 20–
    21, 67–8, 123, 167, 197

IBM 4
impact assessment 147–54, 168
implementation 181, 187–8
impression 91
industry trends 46–51, 77, 127
information capture, business case 145–7
information networks, concept 5–6, 123–4

information technology (IT) 53–70
    future prospects 192–8
    influencing effects 32–4, 46–51
    legacy systems 170–72
    partner selection 26–8, 134–5, 156–65
    personal computers 3–5, 31, 32–3
    platform support 158–9
    project failures xii, 43–5, 136
    scenarios 43–5
    security issues 54–63, 103–5
    see also database systems; networks;
        software; technology
infrastructure review 165–6
innovations 46–51
insurance industry 51
integrators 26–8, 134–5
Intel 4, 31
intellectual property 200–201
internal resources, external alternative
    156–7
international considerations 172–9
    business model 173–5
    legal factors 177–9
    prices 177–9
    product suitability 174–6
Internet
    application development 62–4
    application-products list 9–11, 104–5
    authentication 55–8, 60–61
    background 1–28, 71–3
    bandwidth 193–7
    components 7–15, 62–4, 70, 166
    concept 5–7
    cost changes 35
    demographics 72–5
    encryption 55–8, 61
    evolution 1–28
    firewalls 12–13, 58–9
    free services 34–6, 194
    future prospects 192–8